Dedicated to:

_____
_____
_____
_____

To: _____

From: _____

Date: _____

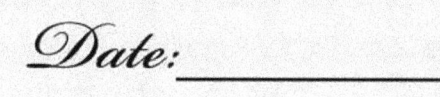
JVH PUBLICATIONS

José & Lidia Zapico

Prosperous… Who, Me?

Discover the hidden power of mammon within the world economy.

Our Vision

To reach the nations by bringing them the authenticity of the revealed Word of God; to build up the faith and knowledge of those who fervently desire that revelation through books, audio and video materials.

First edition 2010
ISBN: 1-59900-053-9

All rights reserved. No part of this publication may be reproduced, stored in a retrieval system, or transmitted in any form or by any means – electronic, photocopy, recording or any other means without the prior written permission of the author.

Cover arte designed by: Esteban Zapico
JVH Publications – Graphic Design Department

Bible Citations taken from The Holy Bible – New King James Version
Category: finances/christian life

Printed by: JVH Publications
www.jesusvivehoy.com

This book was originally published in Spanish under the title: ¿Prospero Yo...? Translation was provided by Ernie Sauve Jr.
ernie@daystream.org

Contents

Dedication 7
Introduction 9

Part 1: DIVINE STEWARDSHIP
1 – Divine Economy.. 15
2 – What Is Stewardship? 33
3 – The Faithful Administrator And The Squanderer.... 45

Part 2: DIVINE MEASURES
4 – Money As A Measure 67
5 – The Precise Measures Of God 83
6 – God's Standard Of Measurement 99
7 – Financial Principles Of The Kingdom 107

Part 3: INVESTING IN THE KINGDOM
8 – Now It's The Time To Give 131
9 – God Wants Me To Prosper 143
10 – The Acceptable Offering 163
11 – The Covenant Secret Of The Tithe 177

Part 4: THE ECONOMICS OF THE WORLD SYSTEM
12 – Deporting Mammon 193
13 – The Economics Of World Commerce 221
14 – Revealing The Hidden Government (NWO) 237

Part 5: TRUE RICHES
15 – Temporal And Eternal Riches 261

Bibliography 281

Dedication

This book is dedicated to all those who tirelessly seek the divine secrets in the riches of the Glory of God and use them in their fullness for His Kingdom business.

> *Happy is the man that findeth wisdom, and the man that getteth understanding. For the merchandise of it is better than the merchandise of silver, and the gain thereof than fine gold. She is more precious than rubies: and all the things thou canst desire are not to be compared unto her. Length of days is in her right hand; and in her left hand riches and honour.*
> *Proverbs 3:13-16*

Introduction

The purpose for which this book has been written is to share the knowledge of true divine stewardship. It also carefully reveals the hidden networks that bind the hearts of those who follow "the system." This system seeks to take captive those ambitious souls characterized by covetousness and spiritual blindness to the point that it becomes nearly impossible to escape its control. There are great spiritual forces that are at work behind money and if people don't have a broad understanding of the kingdom of darkness, they can most certainly fall prey to the urge to possess what passes away. At the same time they will become victims of fear. Why? The reason is that if the system begins to shake, its followers will as well.

It must be understood that the economy is a system that operates in the world separately of the laws that govern divine riches. This world system is governed by the ancient ideology invented by man to discredit the order established by God at the beginning of creation. The original purpose was that man live permanently blessed under the glory of God. Satan through money attempts to control the emotions of the individual to rob him of true peace which is the result of living under the prosperity of God.

Today it is extremely important to be informed about what is behind the financial system and just who has the control of money. There are invisible hands with satanic inspiration that have made plans to control the world; one of the keys to accomplish this is through the economic system. The global elite first planned to build an inflated economy that later fell apart with the purpose of causing panic in the population in people's hearts (they know how to measure human life using the dollar). There is a saying that goes like this: *Those that are trapped by the "drug of the economy" must go to the elite to obtain the cure.* Evidently that is where they want things to go.

The hidden power of ambition and the greed for the earthly possessions is at a high point while at the same time God measures our hearts and weighs our actions. The judgment of God is falling, for those who follow the rules of the "system" as well as on those who live under the freedom of the Spirit. To the latter group, God has prepared the way for them to become victorious people living under true prosperity. Having been totally set free of the control of *consumerism*, they have matured and have understood how to live without being influenced by the manipulative deception it has. By the same Spirit of revelation they have been set from great oppression and false allocations that the lord – god – mammon exercises over the world.

It must be clear that the Lord God is the master of all that exists. Nothing belongs to man; although God has placed riches in his hand, they must be administrated and negotiated with respect understanding the great privilege that this carries.

To have a submissive heart is the active ingredient on a daily basis that generates the necessity of maintaining a living and intimate communion with God through the Holy Spirit. The happiness that most brings fulfillment to the human heart is to fully develop what God has designed it to do. For this to be accomplished, we must have a correct understanding of what we have been called to at this time.

Part 1

Divine Stewardship

1
Divine Economy

When we speak of the divine economy we are referring to the fact that everything we own, although undoubtedly nothing is really ours, belongs to God our creator.

Money is not everything in this life. It doesn't bring happiness, what does it does bring however is what operates in the heart of the person that correctly administrates money and uses it correctly to make the dreams and aspiration of success come to pass.

There are many influences that cause money to increase, remain the same or be diminished. Some of the many things that cause money to

grow and that everyone should cultivate for self and for the family are:
- Learn the art of being a good administrator of earthly and heavenly things.
- Have a broad knowledge of what is behind the economy.
- Have an up to date relationship with God and fulfill all your promises and vows.
- Don't depend on others. Believe that God has provided you with the capacity to fully develop your personal abilities.
- Do not be in debt to anyone (make a supreme effort to cancel outstanding debt).
- Avoid long-term debts at high interest rates.
- Ask questions and take courses to learn how correctly use a budget.
- Apply your intelligence to develop personal abilities.

All of this will open areas of great possibilities. Never let money control your heart, it must be you that uses finances according to the sound guidance of the Lord.

In this life good opportunities should be taken advantage of in the moment they appear, in the right time. An advantage or opportunity could be for example:

- having responsible parents that instilled the value of education in finances
- having received an inheritance
- having a strong heart and attitude that doesn't give up for anything
- having studied and learned a trade or profession

Happiness that fills the human heart is to develop what one likes to do most in life. This is an overflowing joy especially when it comes with the divine calling. To arrive at such a place we must have a correct spiritual knowledge of what we are in God because this takes us to the place that we can live under His favor.

Some negative influences that can produce a poor economy are:

- lack of knowledge of the promises of God
- little interest in the theme
- personal complexes that are unnoticed and or not overcome
- low self esteem
- great economic failures in life
- laziness and negligence

Money

Money is one of the central themes of the study of economy and finance. Paper money and coins are the most common of money today. Also, gold, silver and precious stones still maintain the essential properties of money. (The paper from which a bill is made is in itself, of course, worthless.)

About money we could say is:

- an intermediary
- a natural or artificial consumer good or personal property
- a common medium of exchange generally accepted by society for the payment of goods or services
- used for the payment of debts.

Moreover we can affirm that for something to be considered as money it must satisfy these three criteria:

1. It must be considered a medium for exchange. Money is used as an instrument of exchange in commerce to avoid the inefficiencies of the barter system.

2. It must be a countable unit. The value of this unit is assigned to a good and used frequently to measure and compare the value of other goods.
3. It must retain its value. When a consumer good is purchased it must retain its commercial value for future exchange.

What guarantees the value of paper money today?

The value of paper money should be backed up with precious metals such as gold or silver (this is considered the norm) or in foreign currency. Unfortunately none of these methods are absolutely safe since the real value of money is subject to supply and demand. For example if the mineral reserves of the precious metal would suddenly plunge that would generate a peak in its demand.

In fact, money is the result of a social agreement where all accept to deliver goods or services to others in exchange for monetary symbols such as bills and coins. As a result, what really backs up the money is the sum of the goods and services of the general population, in other words, the Gross National Product or GNP.

The government should prevent any move to assign a value higher that the GNP to its currency to maintain its value. However, the government may opt to print more paper money which leads to inflation and the devaluation of the currency.

Finance

Finance can be defined as the art and science of administrating money. Finance is an arm of economics that studies the flow of money between:

a) Individuals
b) Nations: The individual nations deal with the conditions and opportunities in which capital is obtained, its uses, payments and interest that is charged in the financial transactions.

The term finance comes from Latin (finis) and means to achieve or finish. This term has its origin in the finalization of an economic transaction; with the transfer of money the transaction is complete. This definition about the action of finance opens our eyes to understand that: *"to move money without the use of a credit* card and high interest is the best way to live without pressure."

Excessive credit is what causes constant stress on the debtor because the lender has the right to require payment. To get out of debt and pay in cash is the biblical way to plan personal economy. This completely avoids getting into unnecessary stress. There are some great advantages in the use of credit; however, its excessive use can lead to bankruptcy.

Render therefore to all their dues: tribute to whom tribute is due; custom to whom custom; fear to whom fear; honour to whom honour. Owe no man any thing, but to love one another: for he that loveth another hath fulfilled the law. Romans 13:7-8

It is extremely important to consider priorities and the value of home ownership because if one works hard an inheritance will be left for the children.

"House and riches are the inheritance of fathers." Proverbs 19:14

Here is some practical advice. The priority of every faithful believer should be:

- Get out of debt
- Get up to date with all accounts
- Begin receiving God's blessings, and it's never too late to start.

Why are we administrators and not owners?

To consider this question we must go to the beginning of the Word of God, to the book of Genesis that says: *In the beginning God created the Heaven and the earth. Genesis 1:1*

In the very first teaching the Lord informs us that He is the creator of all things. In this text the word create is Bara' in Aramaic and means: to form, to make, to produce and create. The original sense of the verb indicates this meaning: to carve or to mold as with wood or a sculpture. Bara' is the appropriate word to describe the process of creating something from nothing or to mold something that exists into something new; which God did forming man from the dust of the earth. (Genesis 1:27) God is always the subject of the verb Bara' en its common form. Therefore, to create is a divine attribute.

This first illustration shows us that we are the creation of the Almighty and not the result of a stellar explosion or as the scientists tell us the result of the gathering of mysterious cosmic dust or the evolution of the monkey that by the way still live in trees. The prophet Isaiah with the revelation of the Spirit of God gives a wonderfully impressive description saying:

Who hath measured the waters in the hollow of his hand, and meted out heaven with the span, and comprehended the dust of the earth in a measure, and weighed the mountains in scales, and the hills in a balance? Who hath directed the Spirit of the Lord, or being his counsellor hath taught him? With whom took he counsel, and who instructed him, and taught him in the path of judgment, and taught him knowledge, and shewed to him the way of understanding? Behold, the nations are as a drop of a bucket, and are counted as the small dust of the balance: behold, he taketh up the isles as a very little thing. Isaiah 40:12-15

Also the Lord reiterates in His Word that He is the absolute owner of everything we see, what we don't even know, what we can't touch because it is so microscopic. Because of all this He is the creator of the visible and the invisible of the unheard and the marvelous.

All things have been created by God and given to His Son; they were then entrusted to mankind, created to be administrators of earthly possessions and true riches.

Each person is accountable before God to fulfill the responsibilities of proper administration. It cannot be forgotten that the Lord is owner of:

1. The earth and everything in it. (Psalm 24:1)
2. The heavens and the universe. (Deuteronomy 10:14)
3. Everything in creation such as gold, silver and precious stones. (Haggai 2:8)
4. Every living soul. (Ezekiel 18:4)

The earth belongs to the Lord

The land shall not be sold for ever: for the land is mine; for ye are strangers and sojourners with me. Leviticus 25:23

The principle we find in this truth is that the land did not belong to Israel but to God. The Lord said very clearly *"you are but aliens and my tenants"* God wanted to emphasize that Israel would live in a land that they didn't own. In the same way the Christian believer lives in the land as an "alien" and pilgrim and seeks a city *"whose builder and maker is God." Hebrews 11:10*

Every family had to work the land which was their source of income and nourishment. In most cases if a family became poor that meant that they became slaves, servants or dependant on others. Most toiled diligently to avoid poverty but at times sickness, a crop failure or other adversity could oblige a man to become indebted to the point that renting or selling his property was his only option.

In that case there were three options that came into play:

1. The **kinsman redeemer** could redeem (purchase) the land of the person with difficulties. With the purchase price the creditor was paid. That way the land remained in the family. The poor family continued to live on the land and in time the debt was paid to the kinsman redeemer. This redeemer was the closest male relative, if he could not fulfill his responsibility to redeem the land; it was passed along to the next in line who could. This is the story of Ruth when Boaz acted

as the redeemer and bought Naomi's property.

2. There is also the possibility that there was **no kinsman redeemer** and with time the poor man could come back to purchase his land. The price of the land was prorated according to the years that were to pass until the next Year of Jubilee. At that time the corresponding amount was returned to the buyer. (Leviticus 25: 26 – 27)

3. The poor person could also **wait until the Year of Jubilee** to return to the land of his inheritance. (Leviticus 25: 28) But even in this extreme situation there was still hope that his family would once again return to the inheritance with out debt for a fresh new start. The laws of redemption and the Year of Jubilee are vivid symbols of what Jesus did on the cross for all mankind. That what was lost by our first fathers in the Garden was lost forever and we could do nothing to recuperate that. But Jesus our redeemer purchased that inheritance for us. We were cast out of our inheritance but in the Year of Jubilee we were allowed to return. This is part of the now aspect in the

dynamic of the Kingdom of God. The Kingdom has come to the earth and we are going toward the complete realization of this truth. We wait for this just as any Israeli family of long ago waited hoping for the Year of Jubilee.

It must be clear in our minds that the Lord God is the owner of all that exists. You own nothing and He is your owner. Your family and your family's personal possessions actually all belong to Him and you must look after, administrate and be productive with all that God has put in your hands.

Thine, O Lord, is the greatness, and the power, and the glory, and the victory, and the majesty: for all that is in the heaven and in the earth is thine; thine is the kingdom, O Lord, and thou art exalted as head above all. Both riches and honour come of thee, and thou reignest over all; and in thine hand is power and might; and in thine hand it is to make great, and to give strength unto all. 1 Chronicles 29:11-12

- **Riches and treasures also belong to the Lord.**

God spoke in prophecy through the prophet Haggai and said: *The silver is mine, and the gold is mine, saith the Lord of hosts. Haggai 2:8* The purpose to build the temple was to exalt the Lord God and represent the extension of His Kingdom. David served as a model for people in praise and worship of the living God, his praise frequently began recognizing the eternal God and His complete control over the universe and His great power.

- **He is the Lord over all that exists.**

David confessed that the riches and the honor that he enjoyed came from the generosity of God. His offerings and those of the people were only possible because God had given to them first.

Not only the ability to give but the desire to give also is a gift from God.

Yes! It all belongs to God! The gold, precious pearls and the riches of the nations all belong to God.

- **The Lord is the owner of all the animals and the plants.**

For every beast of the forest is mine, and the cattle upon a thousand hills. I know all the fowls of the mountains: and the wild beasts of the field are mine. If I were hungry, I would not tell thee: for the world is mine, and the fulness thereof. Psalm 50:10-12

The people were not doing God any favor by bringing animals as offerings before Him. They already belonged to God; He knows all the birds and beasts.

The God of Israel had no desire for food but He did have a "hunger" for the righteousness of His people. Although through these texts the Lord shows very clearly that He is the creator and that we enjoy His creation and marvelous acts, He also entrusted man with certain responsibilities to administrate carefully the creation.

God the creator gave the first man Adam authority over all that was created. Adam operated with authority under God's order. He was under His lordship and at the same time received all the corresponding benefits of a loyal subject. One of these benefits was that he was the crown of God's creation. With the responsibilities given to man, the Lord shows that without doubt, He is the absolute owner of all. God as well gave man specific assignments to extend the Kingdom of God through dominion and government.

2
WHAT IS STEWARDSHIP?

Stewardship is the ability to faithfully administrate someone else's possessions or business. It is a lifestyle that differs from the conventional, a style that stems out of being a servant of God that lives to administrate His business on earth.

To be faithful administrators we must recognize the fact and consider Him to be:

1. the undisputed owner and master of all.
2. worthy of our complete submission and dependence on Him.

Developing a submissive heart is the daily action that activates within us the need to maintain a true intimate communion with God through the Holy Spirit. At the same tie we allow Him to guide us in the proper use of finances and to align us with the perfect will of God. Even in this area of stewardship we need to be always in obedience to Him.

What does it mean to be a steward?

A steward in the Old Testament was a person in charge of the domestic concerns and property of his master. To understand the concept of stewardship we must clearly comprehend two important aspects:

1. God has called the saints to properly administrate earthly goods for the extension of His kingdom.
2. Every person is responsible before God for what He gives because He will require each one to be accountable for the use of money.

Let's look at the correct procedures and characteristics of the faithful steward.

- He was to take care of the household, its maintenance and day to day activities.
- He was to watch over and protect the

household so no intruders could enter.
- He was to be a faithful administrator because the finances were not his own and because of this the responsibility is even greater.
- He was responsible to see that under his administration the household business would grow and be productive.

The first time the Bible mentions the word steward is in Genesis 15:2. *And Abram said, Lord God, what wilt thou give me, seeing I go childless, and the steward of my house is this Eliezer of Damascus?*

Abraham had a steward that was a slave born in his house named Eliezer. In ancient times if the owner of the house did not have any children the inheritance was transferred to the administrator or to the son born in the house. This of course was the case of Eliezer.

Will this slave receive my inheritance since you haven't given me a son? Abraham's question is very important since he had received God's promise that he would have his own son to receive the inheritance.

All the children born to the servants under the

household umbrella of the master or landlord were considered "sons." Abraham had over 318 sons born to the servants in his household.

The promise came to Abraham when Sara his wife gave birth to Isaac (he laughs) who would be the only heir of all Abraham's household. Isaac was considered a very prosperous man. This blessing of God also came on Jacob, Abraham's grandson; he was blessed by God. His eleventh son was Joseph, the first faithful steward mentioned in the Bible. Joseph was outstanding as an administrator and was the Prime Minister of the nation of Egypt.

Joseph symbolizes Jesus who was faithful in everything the Father had given Him; he is a forerunner of every believer who is a faithful administrator in God's household.

The task of the steward

What then is the task of the good steward?

- He is the person in charge, the boss.
- He governs the affairs of the household and family business of his master.
- He is the caretaker and tutor.

- He is the administrator of his master's possessions.
- He is responsible for the care of all those in his masters house.

Analyze your life to see if you are responsible in these important areas. God is calling you to be a good administrator of your economy. Undoubtedly a responsible administrator that watches over and is productive with his employers economy will be promoted and for his faithfulness and honesty will be rewarded.

Everything that revolves around this important occupation can be reduced to these two alternatives: faithful or unfaithful. Because of this is it so important how to administrate money.

The word for stewardship in Greek is "oikonomia" which means: the administration of a family or property, the administration of the household or estate of another person. We can conclude that stewardship is:

- The administration of God's economy.
- Intellectual and spiritual capabilities according to one's calling given by God.
- Having been appointed to supervise in

- spiritual or financial areas.
- The position of treasurer or fiscal agent.
- The task and responsibility of a steward in general.

God's Administrators

The word administrator comes from the Greek (Oikonomos) and is formed by two words: Oikos which means "house or dwelling" and Nomos which means "law." We can see that order must be established in the house through the law. We recognize that the finances are within this order. There is another word used to define administrator in Greek which is nemo meaning to distribute food or fodder to animals.

As a general definition the administrator is a manager or superintendent to which the boss or the owner has given the confidence to act on his behalf in all areas including income, expenses, salaries of each worker and even the children of the house.

In English the word administration has a very similar meaning. It comes from the Latin and is a compound word with these components: (ad) which means "towards, direction and tendency" and (minister) which speaks of subordination and obedience. In other words we can say this, he who functions under another and lends his services to another person. The idea is also that he is a servant of those around him. These servants are those for example that distribute food at the table. See Acts 6:1-5.

The ministers of the Lord serve the Word of God to the younger and will be honored by the Father. The deacons in the primitive church served food at the tables, (a function that the apostles had as one of their tasks. Acts 6:1) and had to be filled with the Holy Spirit; their service was honored by the Lord. To serve tables is a privilege given by God like that of the priests who presented the bread on the table in the Holy Place of the Temple.

The occupation of the administrator servant is extremely important in that after the creator, this person has the greatest authority and responsibility within that particular realm of service in the things of the Lord.

The responsibilities of this calling include:
- to heal the wounds of hurt people
- to guide souls in the knowledge of the Lord
- the govern well in the house of the Lord

- to be good stewards of the Lord's money
- to impart the knowledge of the divine mysteries to the people of God

Let a man so account of us, as of the ministers of Christ, and stewards of the mysteries of God. 1 Corinthians 4:1

Every child of God should be a good steward of the grace of toward others. Everyone has received a measure of the grace of God. It is of utmost importance to develop every gift that has been deposited in the hands of every child of God. Let's read what the Apostle Peter says.

As every man hath received the gift, even so minister the same one to another, as good stewards of the manifold grace of God. 1 Peter 4:10

- Each person must watch over, care for and bless those that are close to him/her with the gifts that have been received from the Lord.
- Each person must minister to others according to gifts received form the Lord as good stewards of the manifold grace of God.

Each believer has been given the gift to serve others. To understand this principle is an important determining factor for what we are called to do.

Our society is becoming more and more addicted to the privatization and individualism subtly deceived by egotism, ambitions and the cares of this temporal life. God's plan is to bring growth through proper relationships and not through isolation.

These administrators are managers, trustees and agents that will be required to give account for the use of their gift in light of the purpose of He who gave the gift.

3
The Faithful Administrator And The Squanderer

One of the principles of stewardship in the Kingdom of God is that each one be found faithful. The unprofitable servants (unfaithful) Jesus called wicked and slothful.

By humility and the fear of the Lord are riches, and honour, and life. Proverbs 22:4
Faithful and unfaithful servants

In Luke 12:42-44 Jesus responds to Peter with another question: *And the Lord said, Who then is that faithful and wise steward, whom his lord shall make ruler over his household, to give them their portion of meat in due season? Blessed is that servant, whom his lord when he cometh shall find so doing. Of a truth I say unto you, that he will*

Prosperous... Who, Me?

make him ruler over all that he hath.

Jesus wanted to teach the mysteries of the Kingdom in a practical and simple manner. He used examples from daily life so that their minds had no trouble understanding the teachings. On this occasion Jesus gives answers Peter's question: *Then Peter said unto him, Lord, speakest thou this parable unto us, or even to all?* His answer came in the form of another question:

*Who then is that **faithful and wise** steward, whom his lord shall make ruler over his household, to give them their portion of meat in due season?*

To each of us the Lord has given the responsibility to be good administrators of all He has placed in our hands. In Psalm 8:6 we read: *Thou madest him (that is to man) to have dominion over the works of thy hands; thou hast put all things under his feet.* The psalmist underscores the dominion given by God to man over what has been created; this is a great privilege to have dominion over His creation.

Let's mention one of the defined functions of the administrator as :"*a delegated responsibility to complete an entrusted task.*"

The Faithful Administrator and the Squanderer

> The authority that is released in administration and dominion requires faithfulness and for that reason it is so important.

Jesus referred to the steward as:

- faithful
- wise
- guardian
- supervisor
- administrative
- treasurer
- caretaker in a broad sense
- especially interested in caring for all that his master owned.

An administrator can never forget that his responsibility is double because he is not caring for his own possessions but for those of another person. This is not only caring for things but actually developing and maximizing the value of his masters business with his efforts. We see in this teaching that faithfulness as an administrator brings joy to the owner and the recompense is to be placed over all. Jesus considers loyalty to be of great importance in assignment we do for Him.
And he that overcometh, and keepeth my works unto the end, to him will I give power over the

nations. Revelation 2:26

The word faithful in Greek is *pistos* and means: a person that has been proved trustworthy in business transactions and executing orders. The theme if faithfulness is related to covenant with God. He, God, is faithful because he maintains the promises of the covenant while man must remain faithful and live according to the stipulations of the covenant.

There are several words used in the Old Testament that shed more light on the subject. Some of the words don't seem clearly related to faithfulness. For example the Hebrew word *emet* in some texts is translated as true and truth with the concept of loyalty.

The Hebrew word *checed* is sometimes translated as kindness, mercy and loving kindness with a sense of loyalty. Those who obey the Lord are on the way to demonstrate allegiance and trustworthiness. The Lord is seeking those who make the whole hearted attempt to do His will. These will see the intervention of God in their lives as His blessing rests over them.

A faithful man shall abound with blessings: but he that maketh haste to be rich shall not be innocent.

The Faithful Administrator and the Squanderer

Proverbs 28:20

Human actions and words should reflect the privilege of their relation with God. As in the marriage relationship, faithfulness is not optional. To establish a correct relationship, both parts must respond mutually in faithfulness.

The word translated "wise" in English comes from a Greek word one is that means: thoughtful, sagacious or discreet. This wise person is someone who has understanding that shows practical wisdom in carrying out of business affairs.

Another Greek word for wisdom is sofía which is the clear perception of things both earthly and spiritual, an understanding of the true nature of things.

Another Greek word to consider is *fronesis* which is the ability to put into action a plan and produce results. And this word *sofron* which means level headed, sound mind, restrained, thinking with common sense, full thought process and sane.

The profile of the faithful administrator

> 1) **Faithful with the possessions of others.**

Prosperous... Who, Me?

Who then is a faithful and wise servant, whom his lord hath made ruler over his household, to give them meat in due season? Blessed is that servant, whom his lord when he cometh shall find so doing. Verily I say unto you, that he shall make him ruler over all his goods. Matthew 24:45-47

The steward in this parable is exhorted to watch over and guard those in the master's house so that no thief could come to steal in his absence.

From the above text the word the word "meat" comes from the Greek word *trofe* and has this meaning: nourishment, livelihood and wages. This is more than giving food to children. It is nourish correctly with the Word of God and provide for them spiritually. Let's remember that the Lord was referring to the fact that the steward had to give the nourishment in a timely fashion.

These two things are necessary to become a faithful steward:

    a) Watch over and guard
    b) Nourish materially and spiritually meeting the needs of those he is responsible for.

By doing this, the recompense when the master returned would be great. This is the hope of every believer, to receive a recompense for the services given in this life for others. Jesus said that a glass of water given even to a little one would not be without a reward. In this parable Jesus said what the reward would be:

- **He would be made ruler over his goods.** Jesus would honor the faithful steward and make him an administrator of the inheritance Jesus would receive from the Father during His rule on earth.
- **He would enter into the joy of his Lord.** This means that he would enjoy heavenly blessings in the Kingdom of God through out all eternity. Matthew 25:21-23

2) Faithful over small things

Of course, God tests us in small things and if we are faithful with those small areas, He will add more responsibility. But a more complex experience is when He tests us with money. Few people choose to honor Him as a father and as the owner of all. If the person being tested is not honest while managing a small amount the Lord will never trust that person wilt thousands.

God gives us the opportunity to administrate in His Kingdom riches that are incalculable. There is no way to ascribe a monetary value to those riches. The point here is this, if a person has been found unfaithful or covetous with a dollar, who would trust him with thousands of dollars?

Until the lesson to be good and faithful administrators has been learned, we will not be ready for more responsibility, neither here on earth or in the coming Kingdom.

He that is faithful in that which is least is faithful also in much: and he that is unjust in the least is unjust also in much. If therefore ye have not been faithful in the unrighteous mammon, who will commit to your trust the true riches? And if ye have not been faithful in that which is another man's, who shall give you that which is your own? Luke 16:10-12

3) Faithful to help the needy

Beloved, thou doest faithfully whatsoever thou doest to the brethren, and to strangers; Which have borne witness of thy charity before the church: whom if thou bring forward on their journey after a godly sort, thou shalt do well: Because that for his name's sake they went forth, taking nothing of the Gentiles. We therefore ought to receive such, that we might be fellowhelpers to the truth. 3 John 5-8

4) Faithful with personal administration

The apostle Paul also reminds us that the Lord requires us to be above all faithful in the way we manage our resources and possessions. *Let a man so account of us, as of the ministers of Christ, and stewards of the mysteries of God. Moreover it is required in stewards, that a man be found faithful.* 1 Corinthians 4:1-2

The unfaithful steward

Let's go back to Luke 12:45-47 where we read: *But and if that servant say in his heart, my lord delayeth his coming; and shall begin to beat the menservants and maidens, and to eat and drink, and to be drunken; the lord of that servant will come in a day when he looketh not for him, and at an hour when he is not aware, and will cut him in sunder, and will appoint him his portion with the unbelievers. And that servant, which knew his lord's will, and prepared not himself, neither did according to his will, shall be beaten with many stripes.*

This teaches us that in the same way there is a reward for the faithful, there will be punishment for the unfaithful. We can see the justice of God in this text.

Let's look at this phrase in verse 46: *will cut him in sunder, and will appoint him his portion with the unbelievers.* The word *unbelievers* in Greek means: an unfaithful person, one who has no faith, an untrustworthy person. These two servants who belong to their masters illustrate the two attitudes people will have before Christ's return. The wise and faithful servant will be given greater responsibilities in the Lord's Kingdom. The unfaithful servant will be severely punished, cut in half (this was a form of punishment used in the ancient world.) A phrase used frequently in Matthew is: *there shall be wailing and gnashing of teeth.* This is always used to express the remorse that is felt when one has suffered great loss. Those that won't become diligent servants of God will not receive the blessings of the millennial Kingdom.

The unfaithful servant abused his authority in that:

- he mistreated those under his care
- he entertained himself with personal pleasure (he was drunk)
- he did not watch out for those under his care
- he knew the truth but was unprepared as he did not live according to the knowledge he possessed
- he despised and rejected the will of his master.

The unfaithful administrator of course will be severely punished, first of all because he underestimated the value of his calling and secondly, because he didn't acknowledge the righteousness of his master. Today there are so many that don't believe the word that God gives them personally; they don't hear His calling. They will be judged for their actions. However, God will honor true believers who work and act in truth.

The parable of the unrighteous steward

There was a certain rich man, which had a steward; and the same was accused unto him that he had wasted his goods. Luke 16:1

In Luke 16 shares another parable about the importance of the management of finances, the unrighteous steward. In this teaching Jesus wants to emphasize the seriousness of the responsibility of money management and the hidden attitudes in the heart of the administrator.

This administrator squandered the goods of his master. The word *waste* in this text means: separate, misspend, squander and disperse. The rich man gives the steward the responsibility to administrate even though he knows the condition of the administrator. In the end he was judged for his actions.

We must understand that God is a just God and gives all the opportunity to manage finances.

The waster misuses the Lord's riches. Money that is improperly used stems from an incorrect attitude of the heart that is enslaved to its own wickedness. The bad actions cloud the reasoning and caused him to have to have an unjust opinion of God. *And he called him, and said unto him, How is it that I hear this of thee? Give an account of thy stewardship; for thou mayest be no longer steward.*

The Faithful Administrator and the Squanderer

Then the steward said within himself, What shall I do? for my lord taketh away from me the stewardship: I cannot dig; to beg I am ashamed. Luke 16:2-3

The phrase *taketh away* in the Greek is the word *aphaireo* which means to remove, cut off or take away. God takes away the position of the dishonest manager. This very same thing will happen to all who do not manage the Lord's riches that have been entrusted to them.

The unrighteous steward contrives a plan before he goes to his master to be relieved of his position.

What shall I do? for my lord taketh away from me the stewardship: I cannot dig; to beg I am ashamed. I am resolved what to do, that, when I am put out of the stewardship, they may receive me into their houses. Luke 16:3-4

The steward is not praised for his dishonesty but for the ability he employs to keep going in spite of being caught. This is a worldly attitude and is disrespectful to an authority. He knew that he would be removed from his position because of negligence; his attitude was that of a faithless swindler. Conscious of this, he continued in his process involving others.

So he called every one of his lord's debtors unto him, and said unto the first, How much owest thou unto my lord? And he said, An hundred measures of oil. And he said unto him, Take thy bill, and sit down quickly, and write fifty. Then said he to another, And how much owest thou? And he said, An hundred measures of wheat. And he said unto him, Take thy bill, and write fourscore. And the lord commended the unjust steward, because he had done wisely: for the children of this world are in their generation wiser than the children of light. And I say unto you, Make to yourselves friends of the mammon of unrighteousness; that, when ye fail, they may receive you into everlasting habitations. Luke 16:5-9

Bad administration brings chaos

If personal finances are in a state of chaos you must get them in order. To do so you must first get your personal life in order and line up with the Word of God. If you fail to do so, you will move in a spirit of disorder that can open the doors of a real financial chaos.

No one likes to be told how to spend money. The theme is considered personal and in some cases totally private. Therein lays the

problem, when money becomes literally an extension of oneself. What one says and does reflects what is on the inside.

Lots of people have their finances in a state of disorder and because of that they don't want to hear straight talk on the subject. Few people actually know the spiritual laws that God established for them to be totally blessed. So many people go to church to seeking Christ only to receive prosperity from Him and not to hear how to organize their finances. They want to prosper but not to become alignment with divine structures. Jesus taught the truth about how to live in His Kingdom, powerful principles such as:

- Dominion
- Conquest
- Multiplication
- Material riches
- Enduring riches
- Abundance of peace and joy

When we align ourselves with His will we become witnesses of His faithfulness. The purpose of God for our lives is fulfilled in spite of the obstacles. The flesh is full of desires but it must be taken to the Cross so that only the true and permanent desires can flourish. How many times has the

Holy Spirit spoken to our hearts to give a certain amount of money? But both our thought process and doubt work together to reduce the original amount. This has happened so often that the first number is almost always automatically rejected. Having the control of the final outcome is to move above the heart of God in the matter.

Who is hidden in the heart and has not allowed that presence to be recognized? Mammon very well can be hidden there without the person ever being aware of the fact.

- He is hidden: the person doesn't know it and there is never any teaching about it.
- He is tied to the treasure of the heart; he is the guardian of the money.
- Believers unknowingly live in darkness and selfish egoism.

If you align your life with the will of God, know this: that your personal economy will come into divine order.

Jesus said: *Sell that ye have, and give alms; provide yourselves bags which wax not old, a treasure in the heavens that faileth not, where no thief approacheth, neither moth corrupteth. For where your treasure is, there will your heart be also. Luke 12:33-34*

Teach your children to be faithful

And the things that thou hast heard of me among many witnesses, the same commit thou to faithful men, who shall be able to teach others also. 2 Timothy 2:2

Practical advice:

- Make it a priority to **seek** the Kingdom of God and His righteousness in your life knowing that in so doing all things will be added to you.
- **Serve** God with fear and reverence (because you have begun to manage the riches of an immovable Kingdom.)
- **Sow in the Kingdom of God** that others be blessed and so that the work of God be extended in the earth.
- **Save** wisely.
- **Don't spend everything** and never spend just to spend. Don't come under the influence of the consumerism of society. If you have extra money, invest in something that won't lose its value quickly such as

Prosperous... Who, Me?

land or property.
- **Sow** in order to obtain a harvest in time.
- **Give the tithes** to the Lord and He will make sure that the devourer will not touch you.

Part 2

Divine Measures

4
Money As A Measure

Everyone has been given a measure. This measure can be faith, grace, intelligence or even the ability to manage sums of money.

Different ways to measure

The person who doesn't understand this principle could build a Christian life full of fallacies as he could perceive the departure point as having reached success or having already attained life's dream but from the world's perspective.

The real purpose is to reach for and obtain what has been designated for us in God's ultimate plan for our lives which is already finished. The calling, the dreams and the aspirations have been placed in our hearts by God Himself. All these are part of a plan too glorious to imagine and to get to the place of their fulfillment is what we call "success."

To reach this goal God has given specific "measures" of grace and faith, etc. to each person. To develop to full capacity each of these "measures" we must be able first of all to identify them, and then to take them on to the final divine destiny.

God has given to all people a measure of grace. According to that measure He will require all to give account expecting a proportionate return because each has multiplied that measure.

The word "measure" in the original Greek is *metron* and means: meter, portion and limit. There is another word *metreo* which means to measure and evaluate according to a fixed norm.

Jesus described the Kingdom as three exact measures this way: *The kingdom of heaven is like unto leaven, which a woman took, and hid in three measures of meal, till the whole was leavened.* Matthew 13:33

Remember that the Lord is the owner of all and He shares the portion to each one according to His will. In the Bible we find several different measures such as:

- **the measure** of faith (Romans 12:6,13)
- **the measure** of grace
- **the measure** of intelligence
- **the measure** of wisdom
- **the measure** of lasting riches
- **the measure** of the stature of the fullness of Christ
- **the measure** of rule given to the apostles according to divine appointment to reach people (2 Corinthians 10:13)
- **the measure** of the gift of Christ
- **the measure** of sin
- **Given without measure** is the Holy Spirit as He has no limits. (John 3:34)

The Word of God also mentions that the measure of man is the same as the measure of the angels.

....according to the measure of a man, that is, of the angel. Revelation 21:17

there was a man, whose appearance was like the appearance of brass, with a line of flax in his hand, and a measuring reed; Ezekiel 40:3

You must realize that there is a measure that has been given to you with the purpose that you develop it to its fullness.

Develop the ability of your faith so that your potential in Christ is developed as well and this so that in the end, in the judgment, you will be approved.

God gives a different measure to each individual. The quality of the work, the values and levels attained depend entirely on the individual. Now, about the virtue with which we do our work for the Lord, it is necessary to do all with excellence (gold) because even the way we do our work will be a factor in the way that work is judged.

If the measure that has been entrusted to you has not been developed correctly, you must remember that in the end, when the work is tested, it could be lost.

Now if any man build upon this foundation gold, silver, precious stones, wood, hay, stubble; every man's work shall be made manifest: for the day shall declare it, because it shall be revealed by fire; and the fire shall try every man's work of what sort it is. If any man's work abide which he hath built thereupon, he shall receive a reward. 1 Corinthians 3:12-14

True success consists in getting to the destination and goal according to God's design. Human nature involves so many desires that tend to move people out of the perfect will of God. These will take time and reduce the energy necessary to walk the correct path to destiny in God's will.

The correct way to develop your capabilities to their fullest is to align yourself with the divine will. This will allow you to multiply you effectiveness.

All incorrect desires must be taken to the Lord so they may be modified and aligned with His will. This will allow the true and lasting purposes to flourish.

For unto whomsoever much is given, of him shall be much required: and to whom men have committed much, of him they will ask the more. Luke 12:48

Don't forget this:

- we must give account to God according to the measure that was given to us

- the same way we measure others, we will be measured
- faithfulness is vital to correctly develop what has been measured to us
- we will be rewarded according to the way we have labored and built.

The measures of money found in the Bible

Money was a measure with an assigned value that was given in exchange for an object with an equivalent value. In ancient times an object that was to be exchanged had a value by its weight and at the same time was equivalent to a measure. The balance scale was vitally important because it represented equity and fairness. God sees the balance with a false weight because He knows the intentions of the heart.

Divers weights, and divers measures, both of them are alike abomination to the Lord. Proverbs 20:10

The Bible is a source of lots of information about ancient measures and the different measures and metals used in commerce. Gold and silver was commonly used as they are today for money. In Genesis 13:2 the Bible says that Abraham was very rich in cattle, silver and gold. Balaam was a

Money as a Measure

fortune-teller in Israel who received as payment silver and gold. (Numbers 22:18) Silver and gold was used in exchanges between kings in the years to follow as well as precious stones were used in the range of prices. Silk material, new clothes and mantles were also considered of great value. (2 Kings 5:22) Bronze was highly esteemed as well and is mentioned in Exodus and Chronicles as material used in the base of the columns of the Temple and the Tabernacle.

In 1 Kings 9:14 shows us clearly the exchange between two powerful kings. Solomon and the king of Tyre did commerce and exchanged gold, wood, precious materials as well as cities.

To have an idea of the value of silver in the Old Testament we can see as an example that a hill in Samaria was purchased with two talents of silver. (1 Kings 16:24) Two talents of silver at that time would have the value of 68 kilos of silver. With one talent of gold the candlestick with six branches along with the utensils were made to illuminate the Holy Place. (Exodus 25:39)

The shekel was a measure and could be divided in half, in thirds (Nehemiah 10:32) or in quarter parts (1 Samuel 9:8). The gerah was one twentieth of a shekel as we see in Number 3:47.

The shekel and the talent are both measures of a monetary value. In that time the talent was approximately 34 kilos which was in the New Testament 6,000 pieces of silver, which is some 21,600 grams of silver. The Romans used pieces of copper with the seal of the Caesar of the period as coins for different payments. They also used the talent and the mina of silver.

The mina was Greek currency and was used during the Roman Empire. In the time of Christ the mina was a unit of weight and consequently also used as money; it was used in ancient Babylon and was in use until the classic period with different definitions according to the place and time. We can define the mina as a monetary unit equivalent to a little less than the salary of three months work in the Roman Empire. A mina was equal to 100 pieces of silver and at the same time equal to the sixteenth part of a talent. So we can see that the weight of ten minas was a considerable sum of money.

Its weight in the time of Babylon was about ½ kilo = 491,175 grams. A mina was approximately 60 shekels and a talent was 60 minas. So, the mina was subdivided into 60 shekels and 60 minas were equal to one talent.

Money as a Measure

- **Mina (pound)** – (60 shekels) = ½ kilo (Luke 19:13)
- **Talent** of gold or silver – (60 minas) this could be equivalent to 30 kilos of silver. If the talent was gold the value would be much higher.
- **Shekel of silver** – (un shekel = 20 gerahs) equal to 11.4 grams of silver
- **Gerah** – 0.57 gram of silver
- **Piece of silver** – 100 = 1 mina and one piece of silver was equal to a denarius.
- **Denarius (penny)** – 1 denarius was the salary of a roman soldier per day and was 4 grams of silver.
- **Mite** – 2 mites = 1 farthing (Mark 12:42)
- **Farthing** – ½ the value of the mite (Matthew 5:26, Luke 12:6)

And unto one he gave five talents, to another two, and to another one; to every man according to his several ability; and straightway took his journey. Then he that had received the five talents went and traded with the same, and made them other five talents. Matthew 25:15-16

The Parable of the Ten Minas (Pounds)

He said therefore, a certain nobleman went into a far country to receive for himself a kingdom, and to return. And he called his ten servants, and delivered them ten pounds, and said unto them, Occupy till I come. But his citizens hated him, and sent a message after him, saying, we will not have this man to reign over us. And it came to pass, that when he was returned, having received the kingdom, then he commanded these servants to be called unto him, to whom he had given the money, that he might know how much every man had gained by trading. Then came the first, saying, Lord, thy pound hath gained ten pounds. Luke 19:12-16

In this parable the rich man invested his fortune by distributing it among his employees with the purpose that they would invest the money and obtain an increase over the original amount. Each one of the servants received one pound. Now the mission is to put the money to work and get a return. The master was to go on a trip and upon his return each would give account of his work. The diligent employee should have upon the return of his master 10 pounds. That would give the privilege to be over 10 cities.

Then came the first, saying, Lord, thy pound hath gained ten pounds. And he said unto him, Well, thou good servant: because thou hast been faithful in a very little, have thou authority over ten cities.

And the second came, saying, Lord, thy pound hath gained five pounds. Luke 19:16-18

The lesson of this parable is this: the master represents Jesus Christ who gave gifts and even His own economy to be correctly managed by good stewards, sincere and faithful people. The employees that worked hard and multiplied what they had received would be doubly honored and distinguished when Jesus was to return in His Glory. These would receive a reward of authority and government over cities. This will happen when Jesus establishes His Kingdom over the earth.

The reward of being a good steward brings honor to that person as well as a special position of authority.

He who faithfully maintains his testimony and properly manages what he as received will get a reward. But now with the great difference that honor brings. He will be over thrones; what a privilege because he was once an employee and now he becomes a ruler.

And he said unto him, Well, thou good servant: because thou hast been faithful in a very little, have thou authority over ten cities. Luke 19:17

> **In the Kingdom of God there always must be an increase and production since multiplication is a principle that is in effect since the Garden of Eden.**

Let's look at some of the promises of God given to His faithful people; God will give authority to His children to:

- **Rule over cities.** *And he said unto him, Well, thou good servant: because thou hast been faithful in a very little, have thou authority over ten cities. Luke 19:17*
- **Govern His house and courts.** *Thus saith the Lord of hosts; If thou wilt walk in my ways, and if thou wilt keep my charge, then thou shalt also judge my house, and shalt also keep my courts, and I will give thee places to walk among these that stand by. Zechariah 3:7*
- **Rule over the earth.** *And hast made us unto our God kings and priests: and we shall reign on the earth. Revelation 5:10, 2 Timothy 2:12*
- **Serve the Lord at His table in the temple of Jerusalem.** *They shall enter into my sanctuary, and they shall come near to my table, to minister unto me, and they shall keep my charge. Ezekiel 44:16*

Sit on the 12 thrones together with Him. (This promise is given to the 12 apostles.) *And Jesus said unto them, Verily I say unto you, That ye which have followed me, in the regeneration when the Son of man shall sit in the throne of his glory, ye also shall sit upon twelve thrones, judging the twelve tribes of Israel. Matthew 19:28*

5
THE PRECISE MEASURES OF GOD

But unto every one of us is given grace according to the measure of the gift of Christ. Ephesians 4:7

Give, and it shall be given unto you; good measure, pressed down, and shaken together, and running over, shall men give into your bosom. For with the same measure that ye mete withal it shall be measured to you again. Luke 6:38

These texts refer to the fact that the way you measure to others, it will be measured to you. Even our days are counted from the day we are born. With a certain measure we will be measured, recompenses and rewards will be received according to the measure we have received.

Accountability will be required for to the measure that was entrusted to us, and according to that measure it will be returned.

God has so much more than we can imagine. Only faith can bring us to the place to receive more from Him in both the spiritual and economic dimensions. The purpose of God is that you enter into a level that goes beyond what you have experienced up to now. To enter into that supernatural level of the Spirit it is necessary to break with old structures that keep you from seeing beyond what your eyes can see. For this to happen one must go deeper in the Spirit spending more time to seek His presence.

The purpose that God has in this is that you move beyond the natural realm into the spiritual realm by the action that is called faith in God.

When you enter into the level that God has for you, from that advantageous position you will be able break that which limits you and those areas of the mind that have kept you from advancing. Many of the areas of the mind are marked with the word "impossibility." If you want to reach success in life by reaching your goals, you must break the mental structures of the mind that were forged beginning in your infancy. These structures are like great towers and to get to spiritual heights in Christ, you must tear them down. Once you are free you will be able to move easily into the supernatural realm.

When we enter the supernatural dimension of faith we break off of us what held us back from doing God's will in our lives.

It is because of this that words spoken in faith can bring changes to your life; they can take you to a level higher than what you are accustomed to normally. For the supernatural to come to our lives, every area has to be totally free, this is to be able to access that which God has prepared for you and receive the blessings that are sought after.

God is the God of extraordinary plans. He has planned everything perfectly. Everything that He has done has been designed with a special purpose. Enter into His plan wholeheartedly!

You exist because God has a purpose, you move because of a purpose, you are not an insignificant creature in nature nor a human accident; you are made with divine foresight.

God is a God of order and plans

When we read the book of Genesis we see that the creator was creating something new every day. Why is it that the Lord numbers the work of His creation with detail every day? It is because He is a God that has a plan. People that don't like to order their spiritual life prefer to live their life day by day. They like things their way.

God is a God of perfect and exact measures.

The psalmist asks God... *Lord, make me to know mine end, and the measure of my days, what it is; that I may know how frail I am. Behold, thou hast made my days as an handbreadth; and mine age is as nothing before thee: verily every man at his best state is altogether vanity. Selah. Surely every man walketh in a vain shew: surely they are disquieted in vain: he heapeth up riches, and knoweth not who shall gather them. Psalm 39:4-6*

The measure that is given by God tells you what your limits are and how far you can go. Because of this it is absolutely necessary to know His will; in this will you move with authority within the divine framework. Economically you can prosper and grow into new areas because God is the God of multiplication and forward advance.

Let's look at something: a person goes to the temple and received plans from God. He leaves the temple quite happily promising that he will begin to put them in action. But the next day he begins to do things differently than the plan God showed him. Next Sunday he goes to church and complains out of frustration saying, "What a terrible week I've had! Then the Holy Spirit reminds him about the plans and measures he had to take, but since he had forgotten he did things his own way.

God has to speak and say that you can't lament the fact that things didn't turn out well. (Some people don't advance because they always live in week end mode.) God wants you to advance in all things even in areas relating to your personal comfort.

Learn to do things as He would have you do them. Never ask God why you have to do certain things. Just obey.

Others get desperate and don't wait on God's timing. When they see with their physical eyes that what God has promised has not happened, (looking only based on their time frame and not on God's) without realizing it they abort His plans for their lives. **REMEMBER: when God has**

spoken, He will come through and fulfill what He promised. Don't get the notion that God has to do things your way. Let every plan and every purpose come out of the strength that He gives attain them.

Through the Spirit of God successful plans are conceived. Get into His revelation and your plans and purposes will be easier to accomplish.

God will measure you by what you hear and what you speak

For with what judgment ye judge, ye shall be judged: and with what measure ye mete, it shall be measured to you again. Matthew 7:2

Here we see another one of God's measures. Try to be careful with your words. Be slow to speak. Its better to not be so quick to speak because later God will judge you according to the quality and measure of you own words. With the same measure that you:

- establish a relation with others, you will be understood.
- love, you will be loved.
- give, you will be given.

- speak, you will be measured and judged as the angels record all.

For the Son of man shall come in the glory of his Father with his angels; and then he shall reward every man according to his works. Matthew 16:27

God will not only judge us according to what words we speak, He will also judge according to what we hear. In Mark 4:24 Jesus says: *And he said unto them, Take heed what ye hear: with what measure ye mete, it shall be measured to you: and unto you that hear shall more be given.*

If what you hear affects you and has for example the tendency to take you towards poverty, you have to stop listening. Because you will be measured according to what you hear. You will never get into a level of deep revelation if the only thing you listen to is what is said in the world.

Be careful who you speak to and who you associate with. The associations and the counsel of the unrighteous can be harmful. Don't do business with the wicked or take their counsel.

You need to understand that you no longer belong to yourself, that you must follow the voice of the Lord Jesus and grow into the abundant life.

God is He who reveals things ahead of time; within this revelation is your future and economy. Enter into this dimension where your promised blessing lies.

The scrolls and the measures revealed to the prophet Ezekiel

For he whom God hath sent speaketh the words of God: for God giveth not the Spirit by measure unto him. John 3:34

The Spirit of God revealed extraordinary truths to the prophet Ezekiel in visions. These were about the future moves of God. From the first chapters Ezekiel begins to write about divine delineations and plans that move together with the Glory of God. Toward the end of the book he writes how he saw in vision an angel that had a measuring reed to measure the Temple of God. (It would be overwhelming if God suddenly revealed all His plans for your life, all together they are so great that the mind could not assimilate them all.) God's future plans for your life are fabulous!

The things that happen on planet earth are not without a reason. For everything there is an established order throughout time, these are the purposes of God that come from heaven itself. You are a part of this glorious plan!

In chapter two the prophet Ezekiel writes about the roll of the book that moved. God said that he was to take the roll into his hands and eat it. Everything that God establishes in heaven will be manifested in the earth with **built in order** that was planned ahead. There is order not only in mathematics and economy but also in the things you do and way you move about in your life. There is a prophetic word that comes to life now that says: *"Stretch forth the curtains of thine habitations; spare not, don't be limited. I will give you the North, the South, the East and the West. Reach out, press into what I have for you and be faithful where I place you."*

Every number and measure has a prophetic significance. Make sure that your plan for the future is in alignment with the heavenly plan.

The Bible says that should redeem the time because the days are evil. Why does God say that everything that we do on earth directly affects eternity? It is because everything has an effect and a consequence.

The church should function in the order of disciplines and alignment with heaven because that is the way that the Kingdom of God functions.

The prophet saw four living beings, four cherubims and four wheels of the Glory of God. The number four represents the stability of the projects that God executes in the earth, the four cardinal points and the four seasons within the divine cycles. When God begins to show Ezekiel four movements this shows that in all these ways that God's plans are immovable.

Analyze your dreams and aspirations before the Lord to see if they are aligned with heaven.

When God gives you the responsibility to manage something it is stable, it has foundations, weight and consistency. His projects are always triumphant for man and His creation. Do everything knowing that He will be behind you and will reward you according to the quality of your work. Just as God gave Ezekiel revelation about extraordinary things, in this same way the

Holy Spirit wants to give every born again Christian supernatural encounters and experiences from heaven. Don't look at things from a natural point of view. Look at things from a heavenly perspective where Christ is seated.

Ezekiel's work could be considered as unconventional. The same could be said about Jeremiah, Isaiah and Daniel. You need to know something, when you are called by God, you will do things that other people will not do. Don't be concerned about what they might say; you are called for a special plan and purpose. For every individual, family and church there is a special project that has its origin in heaven. *Moreover he said unto me, Son of man, eat that thou findest; eat this roll, and go speak unto the house of Israel. So I opened my mouth, and he caused me to eat that roll. And he said unto me, Son of man, cause thy belly to eat, and fill thy bowels with this roll that I give thee. Then did I eat it; and it was in my mouth as honey for sweetness. Ezekiel 3:1-3*

For some the roll remains in the air, for others it is being opened and for others it is being eaten.

Obviously when the roll of God's Word comes from heaven, eat it, as the designs, open decrees and plans with which we can walk in victory and

Prosperous... Who, Me?

fulfill our dreams are within that Word. These designs and measures have been given to your life to build His Kingdom as you are a part of Him.

These rolls come from heaven with two purposes: for the faithful they are divine revelation and designs, for the sinner they are decrees of judgment.

Today more than ever we need to know the prophetic move of God and walk in divine alignment. You should know why you have money in your hand and what it is for; you must maintain the holy expectancy understanding the times in which you live and how to act. Leave behind you the old way to measure and judge others! Keep your emotions stable and don't allow the feelings in your heart or what others do to deceive you. You must mature to such a degree that you see the Kingdom of God in its fullness and fully participate in therein.

Every faithful servant that is a part of this marvelous Kingdom will be prospered and greatly rewarded.

REMEMBER: Every one of the Creators plans will be fulfilled in your life when you eat that Word that was sent and you believe it with all your strength. Everything will turn out all right if you move with these plans that have been prepared ahead of time for you.

Blessed is the man whose strength is in thee; in whose heart are the ways of them.... They go from strength to strength, every one of them in Zion appeareth before God. Psalm 84:5,7

6
God's Standard Of Measurement

If therefore ye have not been faithful in the unrighteous mammon, who will commit to your trust the true riches? Luke 16:11

Money is a God's standard of measurement and the bench mark test for our lives.

This chapter is written to consider some of the many reasons and benefits of being generous. God gives money not only as provision to meet your needs but to serve as a divine yardstick that allows God to judge and evaluate the intimate secrets of man.

1) The area that God will first evaluate you with money is that of loyalty.

Do you serve God or that imposter god of money? God reveals Himself as a jealous God that will not tolerate serving other gods. In Luke 16:13 Jesus declares that money is a false god and that Christians can't pretend to serve God and money. The Pharisees were a group of people who loved and served money in stead of serving God. In Luke 11:41 Jesus told them that in order to dethrone money that occupied that elevated place in their lives they had to show generosity to the poor and be free of idolatry. So you may ask yourself, doesn't money reveal the God that you are serving?

Those that regularly give to promote the Kingdom of God are those that in fact serve the Lord while the covetous show who they serve as lord.

---

2) The second area that God evaluates is the heart.

Jesus confirms that the greatest commandment is: *Thou shalt love the Lord thy God with all thy heart, and with all thy soul, and with all thy mind. Matthew 22:37* Jesus also declares in Luke 12:32-34 that where you put your heart is where your treasure is as well, and after this comes your desires and aspirations. Abundantly investing in the Kingdom reveals in itself that your heart's deepest desires are dedicated to in service to God. A jealous passion is required to support all means that extend the Kingdom of God and bring souls to salvation. It is highly important to invest at this time in what is really considered important and special.

When you wisely consider how to manage your financial affairs, you are actually telling yourself and God what the priority of your heart is.

> 3) The third area that God measures in us is confidence.

Jesus could have chosen several areas in which to measure the level of confidence in the heart of man, but of course He chose to use money. The heart is tested measuring in who it trusts, in personal abilities, personal effort or in total dependency in God. The relation between finances and trust in ones personal abilities is mentioned over and over again by king David. *For I will not trust in my bow, neither shall my sword save me. Psalm 44:6 Blessed is that man that maketh the Lord his trust. Psalm 40:4*

> **If you say that you are faithful to God and that you love the Kingdom of God but at the same time don't invest your money in the Kingdom, you are deceiving yourself.**

4) The forth area that God evaluates is in the area of love.

In 1 Corinthians 13:13 we are told that the most powerful force in the world is love. If you say that you serve Jesus above all else, then you must manifest the love of God through your life. In Romans 5:5 we see that when we are converted to Christianity that the love of God is poured out in our heart and that our new nature is similar to that of Jesus, which is therefore a medium full of love. The Bible says that your generosity allows you know if you are manifesting the love of God or not. For example, in 1 John 3:17 God tells us that if one has material possessions and sees his brother with a need and does not show him mercy, how can the love of God be in that person?

REMEMBER: Romans 5:5 shows us that as Christians we don't have simply a human level of love but rather a level that differentiates us from unbelievers; this is generosity which is part of the very nature of the Lord.

5) The fifth area that is evaluated is that of faith.

Have you ever noticed that the Bible gives you important messages about how to live in the level of faith and to continually year for a faith that grows? (Mark 11:23) Money then is a way to measure this important characteristic of our Christian faith. James in the second chapter gives some examples of how works that accompany true faith; two times he uses money as an evidence of what occurs when we live by faith.

- The first example is about helping the poor. (verse 14)
- The second shows how Abraham was justified by his works when he offered his son in sacrifice. (verse 21)

To summarize then, what you have seen up to now can bring you to an important question: What does the way you invest your money say about the different areas of your spiritual life?

- Do you love the Lord or money?
- Do you love the Lord with all your heart?
- Are you faithful and loyal?
- Do you love your neighbor?
- How much faith do you have?

Prosperous... Who, Me?

It is highly important that you deeply and conscientiously analyze these five fundamental questions to evaluate where your true treasure is and what are the inclinations of your heart.

7
Financial Principles Of The Kingdom

Financial Principles within the Kingdom of God

And unto Adam he said, Because thou hast hearkened unto the voice of thy wife, and hast eaten of the tree, of which I commanded thee, saying, Thou shalt not eat of it: cursed is the ground for thy sake; in sorrow shalt thou eat of it all the days of thy life; Thorns also and thistles shall it bring forth to thee; and thou shalt eat the herb of the field; In the sweat of thy face shalt thou eat bread. Genesis 3:17-19

And he called his name Noah, saying, This same shall comfort us concerning our work and toil of our hands, because of the ground which the Lord hath cursed. Genesis 5:29

God designed the earth so that mankind could inhabit the planet and so that the earth would produce the daily nourishment. Because of Adam's disobedience God cursed the earth converting daily work into a painful burden for man. The curse fell on the earth and because of this man had to work with great effort and sweat. From the earth he would get his nourishment but the earth would not help him; because of the harshness of the terrain, the thorns and the thistles would be an ever present agony in his work.

To the previous burdens we have to add the fact that nature itself would arise against man. Let's look at this:

- **The hot dry easterly wind.** *And the seven thin and ill favoured kine that came up after them are seven years; and the seven empty ears blasted with the east wind shall be seven years of famine. Genesis 41:27*
- **Plagues.** *I have smitten you with blasting and mildew: when your gardens and your vineyards and your fig trees and your olive trees increased, the palmerworm devoured*

them: yet have ye not returned unto me, saith the Lord. I have sent among you the pestilence after the manner of Egypt: your young men have I slain with the sword, and have taken away your horses; and I have made the stink of your camps to come up unto your nostrils: yet have ye not returned unto me, saith the Lord. Amos 4:9-10*
- **Floods.** *The clouds poured out water: the skies sent out a sound: thine arrows also went abroad. Psalm 77:17*
- **Drought.** *And also I have withholden the rain from you, when there were yet three months to the harvest: and I caused it to rain upon one city, and caused it not to rain upon another city: one piece was rained upon, and the piece whereupon it rained not withered. Amos 4:7*
- **Hail.** *I smote you with blasting and with mildew and with hail in all the labours of your hands; yet ye turned not to me, saith the Lord. Haggai 2:17*
- **Locust.** *Else, if thou refuse to let my people go, behold, to morrow will I bring the locusts into thy coast: And they shall cover the face of the earth, that one cannot be able to see the earth: and they shall eat the residue of that which is escaped, which remaineth unto you from the hail, and shall eat every tree*

> *which groweth for you out of the field: Exodus 10:4-5*

So we can see that neither heaven nor the earth would be with man. Even though the earth came under the curse the blessing did not have to wait because God's original plan was always to bless and prosper man. But for this the great condition was unconditional obedience to His commands.

There was also a promise that if his descendants would separate the bad from the good there would be blessing. Satan took advantage of the fall of man to further control future generations. The curse helped Satan:

a. oppress man through the daily hardships in his work.
b. blind his understanding to keep him bound to the curse and as a consequence, in poverty.
c. give man temporary fame so he could not attain his true spiritual inheritance.

God gave the law to Moses so that man could live under the God's blessings with the principle of obedience, so that the curse would not touch him. But man was not always fully faithful to God.

> **Man has had the tendency to separate himself from the commandments of God with an inclination in his heart towards evil.**

To understand this let's first analyze what poverty really is. The word poverty first appears in the book of Genesis and comes from the Hebrew word *yarash* and comes from the root word *yaresh* and means: to occupy by driving out previous tenants and taking their place; other meanings are: to seize, to rob, to ruin or impoverish.

This means that it was never the will of God that man be plundered and displaced from his original state in regards to material goods and his position as manager (lord) over creation.

Man has allowed himself to be robbed and most have not recovered what was lost. These blessings remain valid for today and are waiting for man to recover them; without Christ this is impossible, but in Him all things are possible.

The causes of poverty

Of the 6.6 billion inhabitants of the world only 1 billion people live in developed countries. 4.7

billion people live in poor countries or have very low income. Let's analyze the reasons:

    a. The sovereignty of God. *The Lord maketh poor, and maketh rich: he bringeth low, and lifteth up. 1 Samuel 2:7*
    b. The slothfulness of man. *Yet a little sleep, a little slumber, a little folding of the hands to sleep: So shall thy poverty come as one that travelleth, and thy want as an armed man. Proverbs 6:10-11*
    c. Drunkenness. *For the drunkard and the glutton shall come to poverty: and drowsiness shall clothe a man with rags. Proverbs 23:21*
    d. Lack of resourcefulness. *I went by the field of the slothful, and by the vineyard of the man void of understanding. Proverbs 24:30*
    e. Stubbornness. *Poverty and shame shall be to him that refuseth instruction: but he that regardeth reproof shall be honoured. Proverbs 13:18*
    f. The love of pleasure. *He that loveth pleasure shall be a poor*

> man: he that loveth wine and oil shall not be rich. Proverbs 21:17

So now we can understand that:

Poverty is that state of being "driven out" by demons as a consequence of disobedience to God.

Proverbs 26:2 states: *the curse causeless shall not come.*

This clearly shows that for a curse to exist there has to be disobedience to the law of God. In Deuteronomy 28:15 it is written that if the people of Israel didn't observe the commandments they would then be subject to curses. Hunger and poverty is sometimes considered as divine judgment or a prophetic sign.

Son of man, when the land sinneth against me by trespassing grievously, then will I stretch out mine hand upon it, and will break the staff of the bread thereof, and will send famine upon it, and will cut off man and beast from it. Ezekiel 14:13

Deuteronomy 28:48 speaks of hunger as a curse for having separated himself from God.

For nation shall rise against nation, and kingdom against kingdom: and there shall be famines, and pestilences, and earthquakes, in divers places. All these are the beginning of sorrows. Matthew 24:7-8

God's will was to bless His children, because of this the first part Deuteronomy 28 shows the blessings of obedience. The curses are the consequences of not having obeyed God.

Man in his different economic classes

The Bible and even Jesus spoke of the different social classes:

- Low (commoner) and the high (noble)
- Rich and poor
- Slave and free

With all the different social classes of the world we will briefly look at these:

1. **Needy:** These are the street people and beggars whether they be children, youth or adults.
2. **Poor:** These have very low income.
3. **Servant Class:** In India there are actually two of these.

4. **Middle Class or Working Class:** These work with great effort on a daily basis. They have a great sense of accomplishment because they have attained what their generation considers "wealth."
5. **Extortionist:** This is a movement of shrewd people that live astutely at the expense of other people. They obtain their wealth by force, threats, deceit, deceiving and cheating or by contraband.
6. **Rich:** These people have prospered by having received unmerited favor; they take time to accumulate true riches. They feel blessed, happy and have a sense of fulfillment by having realized the reason for their existence. They lack no good thing.
7. **Those that live in superabundance under the favor of God.**

Save when there shall be no poor among you; for the Lord shall greatly bless thee in the land which the Lord thy God giveth thee for an inheritance to possess it. Deuteronomy 15:4

The will of God was never that man live on the street depending on the leftovers of others. The Lord promised to bless His people so that there not be any of these conditions.

Prosperous... Who, Me?

If there be among you a poor man of one of thy brethren within any of thy gates in thy land which the Lord thy God giveth thee, thou shalt not harden thine heart, nor shut thine hand from thy poor brother: But thou shalt open thine hand wide unto him, and shalt surely lend him sufficient for his need, in that which he wanteth. Deuteronomy 15:7-8

It was never the purpose of God that man be turned into a beggar. Neither is it the will of God that a wife has to beg her husband for money to buy food for her children. Our children shouldn't be beggars in their house because theirs is the inheritance. Also, it is not of God that a legal citizen of a country begs, because the governments should provide and be good administrators with equity and equality for all citizens.

In our time there are millionaires begging on the streets of the major cities like New York and Los Angeles. Many fall into the curses of alcoholism, abandonment and drugs. There are also people that have been cursed and end up on the street because of their own witchcraft. (To have money is not a guarantee that there will always be money; the ability to maintain finances must be developed.)

Many people are in house spiritual beggars because they have never found anything that can help them change their position.

Remember: the beggar is always on the street because he doesn't have a covering or house.

- **He is naked:** He has practically lost his clothes and he is hungry. He doesn't work and asks for his bread from other people. He lives off the alms that are given him and he is not willing to return home where there bread.
- **He is sick:** The beggars of the Old Testament were frequently at the doors of the Temple or of the city. As long as that person doesn't change his mentality and assume a different mindset, he will remain seated at the doors begging.
- **The spiritual beggar:** This person is always picking up the crumbs that others leave behind and eats what others give him. This person will not make the effort to receive the Word (bread) on his own from God for nourishment.
- **The beggar** will always depend on others. While seated outside begging, the doors will never be opened.

Prosperous... Who, Me?

For centuries many people groups have had a beggar mentality. Because of this, the doors of opportunity have not been opened because of a persistent mentality of the rich and the poor (slaves). Until an individual's mind changes and the governments stop extorting the people, the population in general will continue to be affected. Alternatives must be sought to change the mindset and change the beggar to an innovator.

So often people fall into generational curses and patterns that bring them into a vicious circle. To move from the state of conformity to another level requires great mental effort and spiritual warfare. For the mind that has been oppressed for years by the spiritual bondage of confusion and self deception to be open to change requires the destruction of strongholds of the enemy's oppression. God does not want you to be poor or depend on other people; He wants you to prosper and live in abundance. Through your work and divine favor you can receive all the blessings that His Word promises.

The blessings of God

And it shall come to pass, if thou shalt hearken diligently unto the voice of the Lord thy God, to observe and to do all his commandments which I command thee this day, that the Lord thy God will set thee on high above all nations of the earth: And all these blessings shall come on thee, and overtake thee, if thou shalt hearken unto the voice of the Lord thy God. Deuteronomy 28:1-2

- Blessed: as a human that lives in this society
- Blessed: with children.
- Blessed: the work of your hands, production and self sufficiency.
- Blessed: over your enemies.
- Blessed: and set aside for God.

God's blessings for His children cover all their needs:

- **Physical,** divine health
- **Spiritual,** from above receiving the riches of His Glory.
- **From the womb,** generational blessings, children and seed to sow.
- **Material,** from below. This means to be prosperous and blessed without lack economically from the fruit of the earth, with gold, silver, precious stones that is part of God's riches for His children.

> The power of a nation consists in its currency, the level of commerce with other nations, the extent of its territory and the supporting allies.

What the kingdom of the world offers

In ancient time the empires were more than a kingdom and consisted in:

- Land (extension)
- Conquest (advance)
- Taxes (imposed on the defeated nations)
- Commerce
- Temporal Riches

Satan as imitator and usurper wants to dominate through his kingdom in the world with everything revolving around one of his greatest allies, Mammon, which draws worship to itself every time someone depends on money more that the favor of God. Money is raised up as a great icon so that all things revolve around it. Everything that Satan can offer is temporal and quickly dissipates. To bind even more effectively the human soul he has great allies such as:

- **Mammon:** The god of money and temporal riches.

- **Leviathan:** Pride, vanity, self dependence, popularity, fame and human glory.
- **Lilith:** Lewdness, illicit sex, unbridled passions, homosexuality and more.
- **Belial:** Anarchy and curses.
- **Amalek:** Living after the flesh.

Man today is terribly affected by these principle allies of Satan, the father of lies; these attract worship to themselves through those who have not been born again. Israel had all the blessings of God to their favor but was on many occasions defeated, robbed and taken into captivity.

The destruction of the Temple of Solomon was the largest economic, physical and spiritual loss of the history of Israel. The nation was left without their most valuable possession, the Temple and the real presence of God. In the sacred edifice was built with gold, silver, furniture made of the very best wood covered in gold: the Arc, the bases and the pillars and columns, the golden cherubims, columns covered in pure gold, massive pillars of silver, copper in the altar of sacrifice, marble and fine fabrics all which at today's exchange rate would be several millions of dollars in value. Also within the Temple itself was a room filled with treasures, pieces of gold, cups, dishes, trays, precious stones and more.

In it's time Israel attained as a nation riches, order, and excellence much higher than any other nation.

Why then was all this plundered and looted? There was so much more: hand carved molding of fine cedar, the throne of the king with its lions of marble and gold? Remember what Israel lost:

- their riches
- their treasures
- the Glory of God
- their freedom, they were taken captive and not allowed to return to their land.

What were the reasons that Israel was plundered?

There were many reasons and it is very useful for us to study them so as not to fall into the same errors.

- **The left the Lord** They chose their own ways and turned their back on the Lord. (Isaiah 1:4)

- **They were idolatrous** They burnt incense to gods made with their own hands. (Jeremiah 1:16) The spirit of fornication caused them to err. Hosea 4:12
- **They rebelled against God** Rebellion is a sin that is considered equal to witchcraft. Rebellion = disobedience.
- **They hewed out their own cisterns** *For my people have committed two evils; they have forsaken me the fountain of living waters, and hewed them out cisterns, broken cisterns, that can hold no water. Jeremiah 2:13*
- **They left the fear of God** in their hearts. *Thine own wickedness shall correct thee, and thy backslidings shall reprove thee: know therefore and see that it is an evil thing and bitter, that thou hast forsaken the Lord thy God, and that my fear is not in thee, saith the Lord God of hosts. Jeremiah 2:19*
- **They stopped serving God.** *For of old time I have broken thy yoke, and burst thy bands; and thou saidst, I will not transgress; when upon every high hill and under every green tree thou wanderest, playing the harlot. Jeremiah 2:20 By swearing, and lying, and killing, and stealing, and committing adultery, they break out, and blood toucheth blood. Hosea 4:2*

- **They didn't keep His commands** *Then shalt thou say unto them, Because your fathers have forsaken me, saith the Lord, and have walked after other gods, and have served them, and have worshipped them, and have forsaken me, and have not kept my law; Jeremiah 16:11*
- **They broke the covenant** *Then they shall answer, Because they have forsaken the covenant of the Lord their God, and worshipped other gods, and served them. Jeremiah 22:9*
- **They stole from God and came under a curse** *Ye are cursed with a curse: for ye have robbed me, even this whole nation. Malachi 3:9*
- **They became religious** and God hated their religious activities. *I hate, I despise your feast days, and I will not smell in your solemn assemblies. Amos 5:21*

The believer today goes after the bread and the fish without having made a covenant with God, without serving Him and without obeying His commandments. This brings them under the oppression of a religious spirit and leaves them spiritually blind. Satan is the thief from the beginning and it is his purpose to deceive; he is fraudulent and crooked. Even today he continues to rob what belongs to the children of God.

Know your rights as a child with an inheritance

For ye know the grace of our Lord Jesus Christ, that, though he was rich, yet for your sakes he became poor, that ye through his poverty might be rich. 2 Corinthians 8:9

God revealed Himself to Abraham as El Shaddai, the God of abundance of seed and multiplication. In the promise of His covenant there is no lack of any good thing because the all sufficient one brings abundance even in old age when according to nature life winds down to its conclusion.

If you are unacquainted with the promises of God in the area of finances you will have doubts about the divine plans God has for you. That is why it is so important to know the principles of the Kingdom, so you won't allow yourself to be robbed by the enemy.

The purpose of our Father God has been that His children possess and participate in the coming Glory. But what does this have to do with the money that I need on earth? If you were the inheritor of the greatest inheritance ever imagined having a share in that inheritance greater than any other, shouldn't you be a good and faithful administrator of the material so you could inherit the spiritual?

Part 3

Investing In The Kingdom

8
Now It's The Time To Give

Cast thy bread upon the waters: for thou shalt find it after many days. Ecclesiastes 11:1

A good deposit in the heavenly bank

The time to possess heavenly treasures is *now*; the time to give into the work of God is *now*. If you are still not a giver, there should be a sense of urgency and almost desperation to begin to give. Waiting on this decision means eternal cost and suffering in the Day of Judgment. Perhaps God has spoken to you about your heavenly bank account and you need to give as if it were a bank payment. He will administrate these funds as you are in the giving period. As you make these deposits consider them as a previously formed savings account.

For example, let's suppose that a recession hits your country, or a war or perhaps famine. If you have given faithfully you will have a large heavenly bank account that God Himself is watching over. But, if have decide not to give, you will have no blessings to claim and the calamities that come the unbelievers can come over you as well since you have not produced riches in heaven.

In the future dark times of great difficulty will come over the nations. But those who have made a large heavenly bank account will have great reserves of blessing which they can claim. They will sense security in the middle of the financial panic that the unbelievers will experience.

In his book titled "Passion for Souls," Oswald J. Smith writes a very well known and admired phrase: *"God takes care of those that remember Him."* This truth is very well developed in Ecclesiastes 11:1-2 that says: *Cast thy bread upon the waters: for thou shalt find it after many days. Give a portion to seven, and also to eight; for thou knowest not what evil shall be upon the earth.*

With all the terrorism, wars, famine, sickness and other factors that affect our society today, what a great truth we find in this verse! We simply don't know what disasters will come over our cities and nations; without a doubt we live in times of great uncertainty.

However, those who sow in God in the good times, when things are going well will reap from God in the bad times. That bank account in heaven will be a wall of protection to face any financial calamity that can come over the earth. Why don't you begin to invest in your financial future now by being a generous giver? That way you will build a strong financial arc of protection around your life.

In Psalm 37:18-19 we find more about this idea of shielding ones self from financial calamities. *The Lord knoweth the days of the upright: and their inheritance shall be for ever. They shall not be ashamed in the evil time: and in the days of famine they shall be satisfied.*

Perhaps the Lord has spoken to you about only having a small treasure in heaven and by not giving systematically you have only reached a few people for eternity. If you put off the decision to be a systematic giver by investing your money in the conversion of lost souls for the Kingdom of God, you will also reduce the time that you have left on earth to build treasure in heaven.

The moment to make friends for eternity is now; the time to give is now.

With the purpose of activating the laws of sowing and reaping, begin to giving now! Remember what Jesus said in John 9:4: *I must work the works of him that sent me, while it is day: the night cometh, when no man can work.* The time is coming when there will never be another opportunity to give into the work of God; the time to give is *now*, before that time comes upon us. Psalm 92:12 says: *The righteous shall flourish like the palm tree.*

The covetous heart hides its treasure

When a heart is not aligned with the Creator the individual aligns itself with the ambitions and vainglory of the false lord. Everything that Mammon has is stolen, what man has inherited from God, he has taken away and stolen. He took the power of riches that never belonged to him. He managed to build a pyramidal system and the multilevel system with the money of other people. In the last three decades he has implemented this within the current system. Many ministers and believers have fallen to the system.

To covet the possessions of others evidently first appeared through the ancient serpent that envied both Adam and Eve.

The greatest impact of this decade is that the majority of people in the world are at the point of losing more money than at any other period of human history.

With all that is going on the Holy Spirit is raising up a prophetic generation of Josephs. We believe without a doubt that this prophetic generation will be used by God to minister and help through the true revelation of the Word of God.

We must be men and women in God that understand what is happening and be ready to be directed by Him covered by abundant grace to walk today more than ever in His favor.

Where do you hide your money?

Many believe that in times of economic crisis it is good to acquire gold to stash away in the ground or hide it at home. What can we say about that? The Bible says in Job 18:10 that: *The snare is laid for him in the ground, and a trap for him in the way.* You might think that this verse has nothing to do with offerings and less about your possessions. In the earth a trap is hidden. Let's analyze this carefully:

- **The covetousness of Gehazi**

We have the case of Gehazi the servant of the prophet Elisha. God had healed Naaman the general of the Syrian army. Elisha never wanted to charge Naaman for the benefits of the miracle (he was conscious of the fact that the miracle came from grace and the power of God). God put a red light alarm in the prophet's heart and he was protected.

On the other hand, Gehazi coveted the gifts that Naaman brought. Without permission from Elisha, Gehazi went out after Naaman and requested the honorarium based on a lie. *...My master hath sent me, saying, Behold, even now there be come to me from mount Ephraim two young men of the sons of the prophets: give them, I pray thee, a talent of silver, and two changes of garments. And Naaman said, Be content, take two talents. And he urged him, and bound two talents* *of silver in two bags, with two changes of garments, and laid them upon two of his servants; and they bare them before him. And when he came to the tower, he took them from their hand, and bestowed them in the house: and he let the men go, and they departed. But he went in, and stood before his master. And Elisha said unto him, Whence comest thou, Gehazi? And he said, Thy servant went no whither. And he said unto him, Went not mine heart with thee, when the man turned again from his chariot to meet thee? Is it a time to receive money, and to receive garments, and oliveyards, and vineyards, and sheep, and oxen, and menservants, and maidservants? The leprosy therefore of Naaman shall cleave unto thee, and unto thy seed for ever. And he went out from his presence a leper as white as snow. 2 Kings 5:22-27*

Gehzai devised a plan based on astuteness and covetousness. How many today act the same way! Only God knows the thoughts and intentions! We must pray fervently that God raise up a prophetic generation like Elisha that uncovers the lying Gehazi type that have altered and twisted the true purpose of the offerings and donations.

The generation of Gehazi suffered misery and poverty for years because of this sin. He didn't give anything to anybody but rather hid it in the

Prosperous... Who, Me?

ground. Not only did he lie but he also hid the gifts; perhaps this is not the time to hide finances but to invest them in the Kingdom of God.

The generational spirits of poverty and misery have a reason by which they have entered to bring a curse. To ask God for forgiveness breaks curses because only through the Cross of Calvary freedom can be attained.

In 2 Kings 7:8 we read the story about the lepers that went into the camp of the defeated enemy.

- **The Lepers**

And when these lepers came to the uttermost part of the camp, they went into one tent, and did eat and drink, and carried thence silver, and gold, and raiment, and went and hid it; and came again, and entered into another tent, and carried thence also, and went and hid it.

Hiding money in the ground is not the way to get out of the problem.

Could it be that we are hiding our money for earthly things? Then, who hides money? The lepers are those who hide money. Where do they hide the money? They hide money in the earth. Those who live with a stingy mentality only hide and have nothing. These texts show the relationship between the misery and the covetous who hide their treasure.

- **Achan, he who perturbs or causes trouble**

The word Achan means he that perturbs or causes trouble; this type of person also hides money in the earth. The sin of Achan is another example of ruin and trouble that comes from bringing that which is cursed into the home. The Bible says in Joshua 7:21: *When I saw among the spoils a goodly Babylonish garment, and two hundred shekels of silver, and a wedge of gold of fifty shekels weight, then I coveted them, and took them; and, behold, they are hid in the earth in the midst of my tent, and the silver under it.* This attitude kept Israel's army from winning the battle of Ai and put Joshua to shame before his enemies.

- **The wicked and slothful servant**

The Word challenges the wicked and slothful servant in Matthew 25:26, why did you hide my money in the earth? This servant was not only foolish and had a wrong concept of his master; he also hid in the earth what was not his. Why did you trust only in a worldly way to manage your money? Isn't there a spiritual way to manage finances that bring limitless blessing instead of hiding it from others?

The Bible teaches that the man who fears the Lord will live to old age and as an old man will no stop being fruitful; he will not have to beg from his children. The good man leaves an inheritance even for his grandchildren.

What will you do then with your money? You should tell the Lord: "There is no way that I am going to bury my money." Money is not meant to be hidden; it is to be invested, multiplied and given to the work of God. Every seed of faith that has been sown will bring fruit. What is hidden is what is received with lies and the spirit of covetousness; that blessing placed into your hands is to be multiplied so that in fact it will be the blessing that God intends it to be.

9
GOD WANTS ME TO PROSPER

*K*eep *therefore the words of this covenant, and do them, that ye may* **prosper** *in all that ye do. Deuteronomy 29:9*

What is prosperity?

To begin with we should say that God is the author of prosperity, because He is the one that gives the potential to advance towards success. Expressed in another way, God allows the fulfillment of purpose for which your project was created, designed and established.

The word PROSPERITY is a visible action over a person. This is a word that we find in Hebrew, *tsaleakj*, which means:

- To push forward (in several ways both literally and figuratively)
- To charge (attack, rush, assault)
- Be good
- Go over
- To be profitable

From the same root *tselakj* we get:

- To advance
- To enlarge (increase, augment) 2 Samuel 22:37
- To make progress (advance, climb, ascend)
- To have success from God's provision. (triumph, victory, acquisition)
- To be productive and effective

Prosperity then: advances, improves and perfects. The word has a very broad meaning and covers several actions, physical, spiritual and material. This fruitful tool is available to those who are under the movement of its action.

God is the author of prosperity because He is the One who created the possibility to advance to success.

Simply stated success can be defined as the fulfillment of purpose for which something has been designed and established before it was created.

It is easy to understand that God is a God that is continually in motion and that His character is the source of the action that "begins with the intention to finish." The wheel turns so that there is another beginning and ending; this is what we call cycles, seasons or times. He is also called *El Olam*, the God that moves in eternity; **a beginning that is connected to the end of a cycle, a circle without end just as the great universe.**

Prosperity then is the beginning of something that continues to its full completion. God did just this with all of His chosen ones. God is a prosperous God because everything He starts He completes and leaves it better. Romans 8:30 speaks of this mystery of God. Paul, speaking about an elect group that God:

- Knew them before they were formed in the womb.
- Called them; in their time God visited them with salvation.
- Predestined them; He gave them a destiny.
- Justified them, through the Blood of Jesus the Father accepted them.

- Sanctified them and glorified them to be like Him in all things.

Success never depends on a start; success is advancing to the goal and at the end to obtain it and maintain it.

This is what true prosperity is in God, to complete the work that He has called you to do in a successful and blessed way.

If we commit our lives to the divine purposes that go beyond the carnal mind, we enter into a dimension without limits; we enter into the unfathomable and glorious riches that are only received by those that walk in the Spirit and not after the natural things of man.

Prosperity is the result of a transparent and holy lifestyle before the Lord. It is clear then that God wants His children to prosper. How could someone refuse to believe this?

With all that we have said, it is important to clarify that prosperity should not be an end in itself, but rather the result of a quality in life of surrender according to the Word of God.

1) Prosperity is more than extreme wealth in material possessions

The greatest honor is to be chosen before birth by the incomparable foreknowledge of God and to pass through all the stages of the divine calling with success and blessing obtaining justification and acceptance by the Father through the Blood of Jesus, to ultimately reign, glorified together with Him.

Prosperity according to the definition of the word *tsaleakj* does not mention the term "money." This helps us understand that prosperity is not subject to the world system or economy and that it is something more than a material thing. The apostle Paul helps us understand the theme clearly when he says: *For the love of money is the root of all evil: which while some coveted after, they have erred from the faith, and pierced themselves through with many sorrows. 1Timothy 6:10*

The love of money is what is evil, not prosperity (because it comes from God). The effect of an unwholesome attachment to money is to displace Christ and replace Him with Mammon (Greek mamonas).

Prosperous... Who, Me?

Generally speaking, to push forward and to be productive means to generate money at the same time; this is necessary to live in abundance. However, we understand that prosperity is the action that brings progress and not the money in itself.

Isn't it true that the ungodly prosper and are successful? Yes, but they do not receive the blessing of the Lord which brings true riches. (Proverbs 10:22) Seeking God can open the doors of prosperity, but pride can close them. An interesting story is found in the life of king Uzziah; he was prospered and received lots of riches during his life. 2 Chronicles 26:5 says: *And he sought God in the days of Zechariah, who had understanding in the visions of God: and as long as he sought the Lord, God made him to prosper.*

Punishment and ruin came to his life because of his attitudes of pride and anger. He took on responsibilities that were not his to take and resisted the voice of Azariah the priest. Uzziah thought that because he had the power of riches and fame that he could enter into spiritual territories that had been reserved for another ministry, the king was not a priest. God gives to every person a sphere of influence in the physical and in the spiritual. A man who boasts of prosperity can commit errors if he forgets that is God who gives it to him.

But when he was strong, his heart was lifted up to his destruction: for he transgressed against the Lord his God, and went into the temple of the Lord to burn incense upon the altar of incense. 2 Chronicles 26:16

The teaching of this passage is about the foolishness and pride of man that can prevent the will of God from fulfillment and cause everything to be lost. Leprosy was the punishment of God for the pride of king Uzziah who had to live in a separate house and leave his reign and everything that the position implies.

If the heart is not firmly rooted in the truth that God is He who gives the ability to obtain riches, when the Lord comes and tests the heart, it could be found unfaithful.

REMEMBER always that prosperity, fame and riches are not always in the best interests of man. Occasionally God has come to see what is in the heart of a man as He did in the case of Hezekiah in 2 Chronicles 32:31. *God left him, to try him, that he might know all that was in his heart.*

He also had another test in 2 Chronicles 32:1 we see that in his prosperity, his enemy came to see him. It will always be this way both in the process of progress as in the short distance to the goal. Prosperity is a result of a transparent and holy walk with the Lord. It is clear then that God wants His children to prosper. How could someone refuse to believe this?

However, it is important to clarify that prosperity should not be an end in itself, but rather the result of a quality in life of surrender according to the Word of God.

The apostle John loved his brother Gaius, a faithful servant of the Lord and wrote this to him: *Beloved, I wish above all things that thou mayest prosper.* 3 John 2. But he added: *even as thy soul prospereth.*

For John, prosperity in both areas, physical and spiritual was very important. Si we prosper materially but we are sick or away from God, that prosperity is in vain.

This word "prosper" in Greek is *eudoo* which means:

- To succeed in reaching a goal

- To help on the road
- To succeed in business affairs

The word also literally means to provide help on the road to success. This clearly shows that divine prosperity is not a momentary or passing phenomenon; it is actually the continual and progressive state of moving toward success and wellbeing. This is applied to all areas of life: spiritual, physical, emotional and material. The Lord is He who causes that all things to march ahead on the right path to success.

Does God really want to prosper and bless His children? This is a definite yes, He allows me to reach my destiny.

We can say then that prosperity is part of the gift called grace or favor given by God to man. Those chosen in the grace of the Lord who know and give testimony that they have received lasting riches are more than successful because they are doubly blessed. These are the marvelous riches and those that keep their hearts pure receive them with joy because they have loved the Lord first and they prepared to eternally receive the riches that come from heaven.

2) Examples of prosperity in the Bible

a. JOSEPH

And his master saw that the Lord was with him, and that the Lord made all that he did to prosper in his hand. Genesis 39:3 Joseph was a man that attained success. From his youth he had dreams he had dreams that indicated the direction he would be going in life. The Word says that God was continually with him. This helps us understand that prosperity is the action of walking and living under the favor of God. He that comes to God, obeys Him and serves Him already has prosperity.

b. JOSHUA

*This book of the law shall not depart out of thy mouth; but thou shalt meditate therein day and night, that thou mayest observe to do according to all that is written therein: for then thou shalt make thy way **prosperous**, and then thou shalt have good success. Joshua 1:8* God gave Joshua the servant of Moses this exhortation:

- The Word of God would always have to be in his mouth.
- He had to read the Word two times a day.
- He had to guard the Word in his heart.
- He had to put the Word in practice.
- The result of this would be prosperity and success in all that he did.

c. ISRAEL

Keep therefore the words of this covenant, and do them, that ye may prosper in all that ye do. Deuteronomy 29:9 Save now, I beseech thee, O Lord: O Lord, I beseech thee, send now prosperity. Psalm 118:25 The promise was that prosperity would come to all but the condition was to guard and observe the commandments. For God's children, obedience is the key to receive the promised blessings!

d. GAIUS

Beloved, I wish above all things that thou mayest prosper and be in health, even as thy soul prospereth. 3 John 2

The apostle John greets his fellow soldier in God's army with gratitude and desires that just as his soul prospers he would live in complete prosperity. Prosperity is not only rooted in money but also in the soul that can be properly aligned with the will of God and therefore prosper. The phrase "above al things" shows us that a person can truly be successful in all things in life. God's peace, blessing and favor come together with prosperity.

3. The conditions for prosperity

We see in the Word of God that the conditions to receive prosperity and success in His favor are that man choose:

- to guard His commandments
- to serve and obey Him
- to love the righteous paths more than money
- to trust in God and in His Word more than material riches
- to guard the heart from greed

The feeling that money and material possessions produces should never be greater than the privilege of serving Him with love especially since one of the Ten Commandments teaches to not to covet our neighbors properties or goods. The psalmist also says: *I have rejoiced in the way of thy testimonies, as much as in all riches. Psalm 119:14* We also find: *if riches increase, set not your heart upon them. Psalm 62:10* It is not profitable or advantageous to trust in material things. *He that trusteth in his riches shall fall: but the righteous shall flourish as a branch. Proverbs 11:28*

Jesus also exhorted:

And he said unto them, Take heed, and beware of covetousness: for a man's life consisteth not in the abundance of the things which he possesseth. Luke 12:15

Charge them that are rich in this world, that they be not highminded, nor trust in uncertain riches, but in the living God, who giveth us richly all things to enjoy; That they do good, that they be rich in good works, ready to distribute, willing to communicate; Laying up in store for themselves a good foundation against the time to come, that they may lay hold on eternal life. 1 Timothy 6:17-19

4. What is the blessing of God?

Prosperity without **the blessing of God** is vain because it doesn't attain the purpose for which God established it. The Lord wants us to attain the riches of His Glory. That means to become complete in Him. *For in him dwelleth all the fulness of the Godhead bodily. And ye are complete in him. Colossians 2:9-10*

The word blessing in Hebrew is *barak* which means: to kneel down, to bless God as in an act of worship. It also means to bless with abundance, to give blessing, to praise and to bless. A similar word in Hebrew is *beraka* which means gift, **prosperity**, generous and gift.

The decision to be blessed and prosper depends on the individual; that is a personal desire to live according to the principles of God. Deuteronomy 11:26-27 says: *Behold, I set before you this day a blessing and a curse; A blessing, if ye obey the commandments of the Lord your God, which I command you this day.* We are seeing a word over and over that is related directly to blessing; it is prosperity. The generosity of God as a gift is His prosperity in me. All of His children that are prospered and blessed are at the same time are true worshippers and the Father seeks these.

There is a relation between he that worships and He this is worshipped just as there is a relation between he that has prospered and He that blesses.

We are blessed by Him and at the same time we bless Him for His gift and unmerited favor bestowed upon us. How glorious this is! In this we see His love expressed to the creation!

In Psalm 115:14-16 we read: *The Lord shall increase you more and more, you and your children. Ye are blessed of the Lord which made heaven and earth. The heaven, even the heavens, are the Lord's: but the earth hath he given to the children of men.* Also, God said to Abraham: *For when God made promise to Abraham, because he could swear by no greater, he sware by himself, Saying, Surely blessing I will bless thee, and multiplying I will multiply thee. Hebrews 6:13-14*

In this text "I will bless thee" comes from the Greek root word that means: to speak well of, to prosper and to bless. Abraham was blessed in all these ways because learned to trust in faith believing.

5. **How can we know when a person is under the blessing of God?**

- God's blessing is seen in a person when everything is on the increase and above all serving the Lord without taking away from the obligations in the congregation. What happens frequently is that when there is more work, the Lord is set off to the side; even more dangerous is when the Lord is forgotten.
- God's blessing is perceived when all is in a growth mode without burden or sorrow; there is an enduring joy. Personal character is not given to quick changes or moods, and anger does not control the soul.
- God's blessing is obvious when all is proceeding well and as a result there is a greater faith in the Word and spiritual growth.

God's will has always been to prosper His children and he *hath blessed us with all spiritual blessings.* Ephesians 1:3

The phrase "hath blessed us" means that He has given us the gift of prosperity and the action of taking to completion our purpose and call.

If you continue to read you in Ephesians chapter 1 will understand:

According as he hath chosen us in him before the foundation of the world, that we should be holy and without blame before him in love. In this divine choice you entered into the gift of:

- salvation
- deliverance
- healing
- prosperity

All this is included in the blessing that God has for His chosen, *according to the good pleasure of his will, to the praise of the glory of his grace.*

The will of God for me is to put every area of my life in order to be able to receive His superabundance.

10
The Acceptable Offering

One of the most important functions of the Tabernacle of the congregation and the Temple was the offerings and sacrifices of thanksgiving and worship according to Moses the servant of God. These offerings were a means of worship, like the sacrifice of the burnt offerings for personal forgiveness and the sins of the people. This restored the lost communion between man and the Lord God.

The principle of the offering

The first mention that we see in the Word of God about the offering is found in Genesis 4:1-5. *And Abel was a keeper of sheep, but Cain was a tiller of the ground. And in process of time it came to pass, that Cain brought of the fruit of the ground an offering unto the Lord. And Abel, he also brought of the firstlings of his flock and of the fat thereof. And the Lord had respect unto Abel and to his offering: But unto Cain and to his offering he had not respect.*

Why was Cain's offering not accepted when Abel's was? The answer is found in the same text. Abel offered the *first and best* of his flock; this teaches us the correct attitude we should have in our heart when we offer to God. Abel decided that God deserved the first and the best.

This teaches us that there are offerings that are accepted by God and offerings that are not accepted by God. Let's consider and analyze our hearts every time we give an offering to the Lord; it's not grudgingly or be necessity because God loves a cheerful giver.

How should I offer to the Lord?

We should give with a joyful heart and not out of necessity; we should be guided by the Holy Spirit. *Every man according as he purposeth in his heart, so let him give; not grudgingly, or of necessity: for*

God loveth a cheerful giver. 2 Corinthians 9:7 The churches of Macedonia give us an example of how to give. *For to their power, I bear record, yea, and beyond their power they were willing of themselves; Praying us with much intreaty that we would receive the gift, and take upon us the fellowship of the ministering to the saints. And this they did, not as we hoped, but first gave their own selves to the Lord, and unto us by the will of God. 2 Corinthians 8:3-5*

When we conscientiously give to God in first place, we know we are giving to Him with a grateful heart and with a good attitude. In this way we are saying that our possessions are actually His and that they don't own us; God occupies the first place in our lives.

We want to emphasize that offerings are our response to the goodness and blessings that God has given us.

Offerings also serve a way to integrate God in the financial area of our life and everything concerning the organization of His church. When we understand that as children of God we are administrators of what He has placed in our hands, we clearly see that with our offerings we return to Him what He has already placed in our hands. We give offerings then with conviction and do so to:

- worship God in first place
- support His church
- gain ground in the evangelization of the nations
- help those involved in world missions
- receive the innumerable blessings of His riches in glory.

A content and thankful heart is a giving heart

Our responsibility as Christians in giving is basically the gratitude of a thankful heart for what God has first given us.

- A vitally important example is that the Father gave His own Son for us. *For God so loved the world, that he gave his only begotten Son. John 3:16*
- Jesus as well, presented Himself voluntarily before the Father as an offering; Jesus gave Himself as an offering for humanity which is an example to give all to the Lord.

This is found in Hebrews 10:9-10: *Then said he, Lo, I come to do thy will, O God. He taketh away the first, that he may establish the second. By the which will we are sanctified through the offering of the body of Jesus Christ once for all.* This giving that we see in God and of Jesus offering Himself is an act of love without precedents. Love also is what should be the motivation to give our offerings as Jesus gave Himself for all of us.

To give with the correct motivation is the living expression of love; this action receives God's approval.

To *give* then is the attitude of generosity in the Christian heart towards God and others.

Offerings for God from the beginning

Vow, and pay unto the Lord your God: let all that be round about him bring presents unto him that ought to be feared. Psalm 76:11

- Offerings in the Tabernacle

From the time of Moses voluntary offerings were established, but also there were required offerings and those for the forgiveness of their sins.

Then there shall be a place which the Lord your God shall choose to cause his name to dwell there; thither shall ye bring all that I command you; your burnt offerings, and your sacrifices, your tithes, and the heave offering of your hand, and all your choice vows which ye vow unto the Lord: And ye shall rejoice before the Lord your God, ye, and your sons, and your daughters. Deuteronomy 12:11-12

Both the Tabernacle of Moses and the Tempe of Solomon were financed by the voluntary offerings of the people. It is evident that God wanted His people to be generous as a reflection of the generosity of the Creator towards them.

- Offerings in the Temple of Solomon

Since the people began to bring the offerings into the house of the Lord, we have had enough to eat, and have left plenty: for the Lord hath blessed his people; and that which is left is this great store. 2 Chronicles 31:10

- Offering after the restoration of the Temple in the days of Ezra and Nehemiah

And some of the chief of the fathers gave unto the work. The Tirshatha gave to the treasure a thousand drams of gold, fifty basons, five hundred and thirty priests' garments. And some of the chief of the fathers gave to the treasure of the work twenty thousand drams of gold, and two thousand and two hundred pound of silver. And that which the rest of the people gave was twenty thousand drams of gold, and two thousand pound of silver, and threescore and seven priests' garments. Nehemiah 7:70-72

As we have said, offerings demonstrated the generosity of the heart. Israel gave:

- the Firstfruits offering of their crops. (Nehemiah 10:37)
- offerings as an act of worship. (Leviticus 1:1-3)
- other gifts and voluntary offerings. (Leviticus 23:38)

The priests received the offerings that the people brought. The tithes were for the support of the priests and the temple servants called Levites. (Numbers 18:21)

It is interesting to note that the tithes were never used in building projects.

The treasures of the Temple

And that we should bring the firstfruits of our dough, and our offerings, and the fruit of all manner of trees, of wine and of oil, unto the priests, to the chambers of the house of our God; and the tithes of our ground unto the Levites, that the same Levites might have the tithes in all the cities of our tillage. And the priest the son of Aaron shall be with the Levites, when the Levites take tithes: and the Levites shall bring up the tithe of the tithes unto the house of our God, to the chambers, into the treasure house. Nehemiah 10:37-38

What does treasury mean?

The word treasury has become a modern way to describe the place that we choose to bring our tithes. It is in the exhortation of Malachi 3:10: *Bring ye all the tithes into the storehouse, that there may be meat in mine house, and prove me now herewith, saith the Lord of hosts, if I will not open you the windows of heaven, and pour you out a blessing, that there shall not be room enough to receive it.*

What is the origin of the term?

The Acceptable Offering

The concept of the storehouse comes in the time of revival of during the reign of King Hezekiah when the people brought their unpaid tithes. So much came in that the king ordered the construction of storehouses. (2 Chronicles 31:2-11)

Jesus and the offering of the New Testament period

Jesus always praised the sacrificial offering and the one that came from the heart. His teachings contradicted the vain religious routines of those who had lost the fervor of intimate worship. In Luke 21:1-4 Jesus praised the widow that gave everything she had. Even though the rich had given more money, Jesus valued her offering as greater because she didn't give of what was left over, but as the only thing she had.

In the New Testament **the tithe** was not invalidated. We see an attitude of generosity in people of the time. The question was not a matter of a minimum amount for the offering, but the opposite. In the primitive church the tithes and offerings allowed for the establishment and expansion of the work of God. In the same way, today we all have the opportunity to obey the

Lord with our tithes and offerings. The church of today should be characterized by a similar work and attitude of the churches of Macedonia that the apostle Paul mentioned in 2 Corinthians.

How the primitive church was economically sustained

The first Christians also tithed as this was a aspect of the daily life of the Jewish people. In the book of Hebrews, (written 65 years into our time) we read: *And there men that die receive tithes. Hebrews 7:8* Here the words *"and here"* mean in Greek literally: in this same place. This brings the tithe to time and place of the church. In other words, the Christians tithed in their local congregations where they received their spiritual nourishment. They were also generous and gave offerings to their brethren in other places that had needs.

The believers whole heartedly brought their gifts to the leaders for the support of the ministry. (Acts 4:32-37) When the apostle wrote to the Philippians, he emphasized that the people had given much more than was expected of them. Paul encouraged them in that because of their generosity they would lack nothing. (Philippians 4:18-19)

The apostle Paul taught that the support of the church was similar to that of Israel in its time.

With the tithes and offerings of the believers the different aspects of the ministry were sustained. *Do ye not know that they which minister about holy things live of the things of the temple? and they which wait at the altar are partakers with the altar? Even so hath the Lord ordained that they which preach the gospel should live of the gospel. 1 Corinthians 9:13-14*

We consider that this is a basic biblical principle for the support of church ministry in stead of a legalistic requirement. There will be times when we want to give specific offerings for needs that arise. It is not a matter of thinking in the minimum amount to give as if the pressure to give is what moves us.

In 2 Corinthians 9:7 we read: *Every man according as he purposeth in his heart, so let him give; not grudgingly, or of necessity: for God loveth a cheerful giver.* In verse 6 we read that if we sow sparingly we will also reap sparingly. However, if we sow bountifully we will also reap bountifully, according to what is written. The Lord will respond with multiple blessings for us according to His promises.

What is our responsibility now?

Based on the scriptures that we have cited, we have seen that as members of the church, we have the responsibility to support the ministry and help others. We should always be open to the leading to the Holy Spirit in this so we can know how much to give and do so with a grateful heart.

The more we give the more we will receive. We don't give grudgingly; we give by the guidance of the Holy Spirit, we sow, we tithe, we give offerings, we help in world missions, we give to the needy according to our income and all this to extend the Kingdom of God throughout the nations.

11
THE COVENANT SECRET OF THE TITHE

Investing in the Kingdom of God
...I give tithes of all that I possess. Luke 18:12

The plan for prosperity includes the tithe

Many people are disabled by their own poverty and this is frequently caused by their disobedience to God. This disobedience manifests itself in many ways, one way is robbing God!

Will a man rob God? Yet ye have robbed me. But ye say, Wherein have we robbed thee? In tithes and offerings. Malachi 3:8 This passage clearly tells us that those who retain their tithes and offerings are robbing God. As a consequence, they are depriving themselves of the blessings that God wants to give them. When we cease to tithe or give offerings, this constitutes a violation of a divine principle and the promise of prosperity cannot work to our favor.

Nothing could cause a wise believer to stop giving offerings or tithes. But at the same time, it is understood that giving the tithe is not with the objective to obtain something from God. But rather, the action of giving proceeds from obedience to the principles given by God. He always rewards obedience! *Give, and it shall be given unto you; good measure, pressed down, and shaken together, and running over, shall men give into your bosom. For with the same measure that ye mete withal it shall be measured to you again.* Luke 6:38

Your tithe opens the gates of heaven for you and stops the devourer from destroying your fruit. In this passage of scripture, God invites His people to prove Him through tithes and offerings so they can verify His faithfulness. The text also says that to retain your tithes you put the brakes on God. This keeps you from enjoying the great and abundant blessings that are available to be poured out on your life and on all those who are willing to obey His Word. The prophecy in

Malachi gives a call to renew our offerings based on divine promise.

Bring ye all the tithes into the storehouse, that there may be meat in mine house, and prove me now herewith, saith the Lord of hosts, if I will not open you the windows of heaven, and pour you out a blessing, that there shall not be room enough to receive it. Malachi 3:10

1. There will be "meat" or resources for the work of God, for the House of God.
2. Those who give their offerings will be in a position to receive great and abundant blessings. You can experience the open windows of heaven to pour out blessings that can't be contained, meaning that can't be carried in your arms.
3. God will rebuke the devourer for our sakes. The blessings that are destined for you will not be detained by Satan. Don't be afraid to test God with your offerings; He is the Lord and will pass the test.

Be not deceived; God is not mocked: for whatsoever a man soweth, that shall he also reap. For he that soweth to his flesh shall of the flesh reap corruption; but he that soweth to the Spirit shall of the Spirit reap life everlasting. Galatians 6:7-8

Our responsibility to give to God

Our responsibility as Christians in reference to giving is basically the commandment of the Lord Jesus when He said: *But seek ye first the kingdom of God, and his righteousness; and all these things shall be added unto you. Matthew 6:33*

To seek the Kingdom of God is to seek His perfect will. This necessarily means renouncing self and giving of ourselves. The vitally important example we have is when the Father gave His Son for us: *For God so loved the world, that he gave his only begotten Son, that whosoever believeth in him should not perish, but have everlasting life. John 3:16*

The act of the Father giving His Son is an act of love without precedents. Love is what should empower us to give as God gave of Himself.

To give with the correct motivation is the living expression of love.

To give is an attitude of generosity in the Christian toward God and others. However, there are obligations in the area of giving that we should pay close attention to, one of those areas is the tithe.

What is the tithe?

The tithe simply means the quantity or measure that the people of God returned to Him of everything He had given them. The tithe is holy and belongs to God. The best way to tithe is to separate the tenth of all your earnings whether it be money or products when you receive your income and give it to what you recognize as the church of God.

We keep the 90% and we give God the tenth. This act of faith allows God to superabundantly bless the 90% of our finances. Do it with joy remembering that God is your Creator and Redeemer and that in so doing, you are simply returning what belongs to Him. Return the tithe as an act of worship. Accept Him as Lord of every area of your life.

And all the tithe of the land, whether of the seed of the land, or of the fruit of the tree, is the Lord's: it is holy unto the Lord. Leviticus 27:30

The tithe is an act of loyalty recognizing God as the owner of our material possessions and our lives.

Prosperous... Who, Me?

When does the tithe appear for the first time in the Bible?

The word tithe appears for the first time in the Bible in Genesis 14:17-20. *And the king of Sodom went out to meet him after his return from the slaughter of Chedorlaomer, and of the kings that were with him, at the valley of Shaveh, which is the king's dale. And Melchizedek king of Salem brought forth bread and wine: and he was the priest of the most high God. And he blessed him, and said, Blessed be Abram of the most high God, possessor of heaven and earth: And blessed be the most high God, which hath delivered thine enemies into thy hand. And he gave him tithes of all.* Abraham gave the king of Salem (Jerusalem) the tithe of the spoils of battle that were obtained as a result of the battle with the five kings.

What does the word "spoil" mean?

This word comes from the Hebrew root word *baz* and means to plunder. What was the reward in winning a battle? It was the right to plunder and take the spoils of war after the battle.

God has promised to bless the work of our hands but too often the enemy comes to rob the seed.

This example of Abraham reveals to us that to plunder the enemy (what he has stolen from us) and the giving of the tithe sometimes becomes a battle we have to win.

To whom also Abraham gave a tenth part of all; first being by interpretation King of righteousness, and after that also King of Salem, which is, King of peace; Without father, without mother, without descent, having neither beginning of days, nor end of life; but made like unto the Son of God; abideth a priest continually. Hebrews 7:2-3

And verily they that are of the sons of Levi, who receive the office of the priesthood, have a commandment to take tithes of the people according to the law, that is, of their brethren, though they come out of the loins of Abraham. And here men that die receive tithes; but there he receiveth them, of whom it is witnessed that he liveth. And as I may so say, Levi also, who receiveth tithes, payed tithes in Abraham. Hebrews 7:5, 8-9

The tithe is also mentioned in Genesis 28:10-22. Jacob, after his encounter wrestling with the angel decided to give the Lord **the tithe** of everything he had; *and of all that thou shalt give me I will surely give the tenth unto thee.* (verse 22) This is evidence that when there is an encounter with God, the Holy Spirit gives us conviction that we should give to Him as a sign of gratitude for all the favors received from Him. This allows us to understand that there was a principle of the tithe long before the dispensation or the period of the Law of Moses. This was a sense that was in the hearts of those who truly had an experience with the Lord.

A personal encounter with the Lord will give you the conviction to tithe with joy and happiness.

The law of the offerings and tithes were given to Moses on Mount Sinai when the divine laws of the construction of the Tabernacle were being established.

REMEMBER, Abraham was not blessed because he tithed but because he believed God. Prosperity is what is added to us for seeking the Kingdom first.

How were the tithes used in the Old Testament?

Just as God instructed Israel in things relating to worship and how to live according to the will of

God, He also taught them about economics. How to manage money is such an important subject, No one should be shocked about this! These instructions are faithful and true; they bring multiplication and blessing to all those who put them in practice. In Deuteronomy 8:6 the Lord gives a warning to His people: *Therefore thou shalt keep the commandments of the Lord thy God, to walk in his ways, and to fear him.* In the ways of God we find instruction on how to correctly order our finances.

Actually, money is far from being a just a materialistic subject. It is much more spiritual than it seems. We must not forget that it is related to the treasure of the heart.

The Lord established a principle in the book of Leviticus when he taught the people how to use the resources He had given. God doesn't forget His promises. He always follows the indications of His previous agreements and if man fulfills his part of the responsibility, He will honor His Word.

And all the tithe of the land, whether of the seed of the land, or of the fruit of the tree, **is the Lord's: it is holy unto the Lord.** *And concerning the tithe of the herd, or of the flock, even of whatsoever passeth*

under the rod, the tenth shall be holy unto the Lord.
Leviticus 27: 30, 32

The tithe belongs to the Lord; in other words, we are not giving anything to the Lord when we tithe. We are simply *returning* what already belongs to Him. Because of this, when we read in Malachi the whole nation as well as every individual had robbed God, not only in tithes but also in offerings. Even though we all have different levels of resources and finances, we are all called to be faithful administrators of what God has deposited in our hands. Our responsibility to the Lord should not be taken as something distressing painful but as a privilege to be involved in the process of advancing the work of God together.

We also see in the passage in Malachi that when we are faithful tithing and giving offerings, God is faithful to bless us abundantly: *prove me now herewith, saith the Lord of hosts, if I will not open you the windows of heaven, and pour you out a blessing, that there shall not be room enough to receive it.* When we take to step of faith to tithe and give offerings according to the will of God with a joyful heart, He will have the freedom to *open you the windows of heaven, and pour you out a blessing, that there shall not be room enough to receive it.*

The importance of the tithe

The principle reasons that God has given the tithe system are to that:

- God would have the freedom to bless us.
- God would be vitally connected to our finances.
- We would have the opportunity to worship and honor Him.

He is the owner of all that He has placed in our hands. Every time that we tithe our income we recognize that He has placed everything in our hands. In 1 Chronicles 29 when the people of God had the privilege and challenge build the Temple, David prayed to God recognizing that *all things come of thee, and of thine own have we given thee.* (Verse 14)

Remember, the tithe belongs to God and therefore:

- it is not ours
- it must not be retained
- it must not be used according to our own criteria
- it must not be used for oneself

- it must not be used to support activities such as vacations, gifts, Christmas or at will.

Always keep in mind that your offerings prove God, they open the windows of heaven and neutralize the work of the devourer.

God invites His people to *prove Him* through offerings to verify His faithfulness. God says that when offerings are kept in hand we are preventing Him from pouring out His great and abundant blessings.

He is calling you today to renew your commitment to honor Him with your offerings with a promise; God declares the following:

1. There will be resources for the divine work, the house of God.
2. Those that tithe and give offerings align themselves to receive the abundant blessings.
3. God Himself will rebuke the devourer for our cause.

Dare to believe God and you will experience the joy of being truly prosperous.

PART 4

THE ECONOMICS OF THE WORLD SYSTEM

12
Deporting Mammon
How To Discover Which God We Love

Unfortunately, human beings love to hear what exalts self and anything that brings increase in personal economics to have a solid platform in life. For years in the United States seminars are given with the objective of strengthening the ego and building self-confidence. This false sense of confidence brings the listeners to believe and trust in their own personal abilities.

Clearly, when something is occupying first place in self-confidence even ahead of God, it is *an intruder that must be detected and removed.* That intruder seeks to be first in the mind to:

- distract and not allow to focus on divine purposes.

- take peace and bring worry.
- make one anxious and preoccupied.
- think only in debts and live under constant tension.
- cause anger and family quarrels all which later produce sickness.

To know what secretly moves behind all this and analyze the heart, these questions should be asked:

- Who do I trust (rest and believe in) when the economic crisis comes?
- Who is my refuge when I lose something of value?
- Who is my security?
- When I have nothing to eat, who will give me more security, money or in a daily provision?
- How important are my savings to me? Do I really believe that they represent my future wellbeing?
- Do I trust 100% in Social Security or in a life insurance policy?

These questions certainly reveal the hidden truth of what is in the human heart. Someone might say: "I don't really trust in anyone or in anything in particular, I just trust in my own work." But, is that really the case in life's most critical moment?

There is a daily battle to determine what master we will serve

The fleshly appetites are dazzled by the so called good life, comforts and luxury. Who doesn't like nice things? The apostle Paul said: *Not that I speak in respect of want: for I have learned, in whatsoever state I am, therewith to be content. I know both how to be abased, and I know how to abound: every where and in all things I am instructed both to be full and to be hungry, both to abound and to suffer need. I can do all things through Christ which strengtheneth me. Notwithstanding ye have well done, that ye did communicate with my affliction. Philippians 4:11-14*

Jesus was very radical in His ministry when He referred to this theme. In Mark 4:19 Jesus gives three aspects that cause the true meaning of the Word to be choked in the Parable of the Sower:

1. Deceitfulness of riches
2. Cares of this world
3. Covetousness for other things (that are not necessarily the the will of God).

Rest in the Lord, and wait patiently for him: fret not thyself because of him who prospereth in his way, because of the man who bringeth wicked devices to pass. Psalm 37:7

Jesus was referring to the fact that if a person doesn't have a clear concept of the use of **temporal riches**, the risk is to fall into a spirit of deception. (Deception takes the mind of the person that doesn't realize it is under its influence.) This opens the door for an unhealthy desire for temporal riches and desperation to attain the same level of success that other have attained.

It would seem sometimes that only the ungodly prosper. But in Psalm 37:7-9 David reminds us that those who have strayed from the correct path that God has drawn for us will, will come to their destruction. The prosperity of the wicked is only for a time.

God, through an angel exhorts the Church to be spiritually rich so each person would prosper more and more through spiritual gold that is His holiness, presence and nature.

Revelation 3:18-19 says: *I counsel thee to buy of me gold tried in the fire, that thou mayest be rich;*

and white raiment, that thou mayest be clothed, and that the shame of thy nakedness do not appear; and anoint thine eyes with eyesalve, that thou mayest see. As many as I love, I rebuke and chasten: be zealous therefore, and repent.

Carefully analyzing this we can understand what moves in the heart behind striving for riches and false security.

Without a doubt it is the excessive confidence in money; that which apparently give happiness.

This is the false god that takes the true God from first place, he is called Mammon.

We should know how well it was said in Job 24:23 that God is the only one who gives true security and confidence. Also in Psalm 78:53 we find: *And he led them on safely, so that they feared not: but the sea overwhelmed their enemies.* Daily repentance is one of the keys of the Christian life. Running to the Cross to die to the fleshly desires and natural ambitions is still the challenge given to us by the Lord and continues to be the best option.

Mammon, the lord and god of temporal riches

In the Bible the word mammon is sometimes translated as "money" some versions but in the original it is the Greek word *mamonas* which means:

- confidence
- confidence in your own riches
- relying on and having security in self for the present or future.

In the English Bible (KJV) the word *mamonas* is found in three texts of the New Testament.

1. Matthew 6:24: *No man can serve two masters: for either he will hate the one, and love the other; or else he will hold to the one, and despise the other. Ye cannot serve God and mammon.*
2. Luke 16:9: *And I say unto you, Make to yourselves friends of the mammon of unrighteousness; that, when ye fail, they may receive you into everlasting habitations.*
3. Luke 16:11, 13: *If therefore ye have not been faithful in the unrighteous mammon, who will commit to your trust the true riches? No servant can serve two masters: for either he will hate the one, and love the other; or else*

he will hold to the one, and despise the other. Ye cannot serve God and mammon.

Mammon represents the confidence in what we can have as humanly visible and tangible as in money; this idea even extends to what is necessary in life such as food and clothing.

Everything depends on who your owner is. How can we distinguish what is right in our hearts?

- Mammon is the opposite of believing in God; you either believe in God or Mammon. (This is similar to the spirit of doubt, for example, that hides as not to be discovered.)
- Mammon is the opposite of trusting in God; you either trust in God or you trust in Mammon. (The spirit of unbelief is a more powerful stronghold.)
- Mammon occupies the heart and displaces God. (He can't be first or the second.)
- He steals your faith in God. Mammon steals your confidence and says "I am he that gives you the power through money." (He is the spirit of worry."
- Mammon wants to be the owner of your dreams, ambitions, work, vacations, take your peace and take over your mind. (He

works with and is related to the spirit of distraction and entertainment.)
- He makes you feel self confident. (He takes over "self" as to position himself as god of that person.)
- He doesn't allow anyone to counsel you about the way you use money. (The person believes that money is his own exclusive possession; Mammon is possessive.)
- He doesn't like you to give offerings to God. He prefers that you use money on food and entertainment.
- Mammon pressures the nerves of the stomach when there is talk about tithing and giving.

Mammon seeks to establish himself firmly in the treasure chest of the heart so that from there he can:

- interweave himself with the money
- control what should or should not be spent
- rob from God and use the money on personal pleasure
- make sure that when you give offerings and tithes you are always robbing God and His Kingdom of what belongs only to God. (Mammon knows that this is the way God will prosper your life.)

It is necessary to do a self check up every now and then to see who is in the lead.

- What do you have in the treasure chest of the heart?
- What worries you the most?
- Who has the last word in the decisions you make?
- Who is first?

To understand how Mammon displaced God from the heart of man and to position himself there, we must go back to the beginning of creation. The devil altered the structure deceiving Adam and Eve presenting them with *"new ideologies."* These put doubt especially in Eve (who was weaker and more curious possibly because God didn't give her instructions directly but gave them to Adam.) The enemy very subtly had to teach them a new way to think that denied the truth of God.

The word ideology has the same meaning as ideas. The enemy used "new concepts" (concepts with structures). Today he uses the same technique to deceive mankind.

The precept comes before the structure. Adam and Eve accepted the new structure when they disobeyed the law of God. They left behind the

original structure which was the Glory of God in their lives.

Satan managed to get into the system of man and this altered the structure given by God. He brought "new concepts" and placed doubt in Eve. These doubts broke the structure of God and instated "chaos" which was to completely change the ideology of man. God, the Creator sacrificed animals to cover Adam and Eve's sin and disobedience; He made them clothing of animal skin to cover their sin.

Because of this the system of offerings of sacrifice was established in the Tabernacle to cover guilt. Christ, the Last Adam, brought the destruction of the curse of sin to establish the change in man by shedding His blood on the Cross. Now, man could be part of the Kingdom of God by the new birth.

This brought tremendous benefits for man such as:

- Now he could change his way of thinking. Renewing his thoughts and tearing down the arguments in his mind. (Romans 12:1-2)
- Now he could change the structures of the human system. When the good news of

salvation is taken with the Kingdom of God, there are changes in the human heart; neighborhoods are changes, new job positions are opened and new churches are established. The Kingdom advances with power.

Jesus Christ brought order and structure into world chaos. He is the restorer and builder of order because chaos and disorder were established by the prince of this world.

The secret is to learn to put our lives under the order of God. The result of this order will bring true blessing.

Prosperity functions when we break away from disorder and properly administrate heavenly things. It's like taking the yoke that Jesus offered us. *My yoke is easy*, Jesus said. It is much easier to carry that yoke than the disorder that the enemy offers. (Matthew 11:28-30)

The yoke of bondage is the opposite of the yoke of Jesus. To be a slave of sin is to live under the curse of death and oppressed by the law of Mammon. If you take on the yoke of Christ, you are free of the chains of oppression. With Christ things are so much better!

> **A yoke means to unite two with the purpose of advancing in the same direction. If one is yoked to sin then the direction is towards death.**

When you think about it, being a servant of Jesus is much better than being a servant of Mammon (which brings only bondage and death). What's more is that service in Christ brings honor and eternal life.

> **The yoke of order and structure is much easier to carry than the yoke of disorder and chaos. Chaos and disorder is synonymous with Mammon.**

God's Word is true and righteous; because of this it is necessary that what is unstable must disappear. What is solid and firm in the end is the only thing that will last.

Jesus and anxiety

Jesus in Matthew chapter 6 brings a complete discourse about worry and anxiety of this life and applies it to the true meaning of food and clothing. In fact there are two analogies that are very important to apply in life. Jesus begins to exhort His listeners to be careful of self righteousness before people. About the word righteousness, Jesus was referring to everything relating to "human righteousness" which has to do with personal accomplishments, dedication and human effort.

Many will ask themselves based on this biblical truth, what about the future here on earth? Believing that if they dedicate more time to spiritual things to have "treasures in heaven" how will they provide and make for a secure future? Others might think how can I live the true Christian life and please God without worrying about material things?

Jesus establishes several principles that keep us from falling into the hands of anxiety and the love of temporal riches which are:

- Have faith, because in the life that depends on God there is security. Jesus declares to you *take no thought for your life.* The power in the phrase is seen more clearly in the original Greek which carries the idea that there should be no distraction or anxiety about food and clothing; one should not get to the point of being distracted from the important priorities in life.

- Jesus established that the body is more important than food and clothing. God is powerful enough to provide for life, for the body; this indicates that He is sufficient to sustain the life He created. Since He created life, He is able to provide the nourishment that life that has its origin in Him. He that has manifested His power to adequately form your body is the same one who has committed Himself to bless it. One of these favors is to provide for clothing to cover your body.
- *Behold the fowls of the air*...the Lord is asking: *Are ye not much better than they?* The birds are a real example of the capacity of God to provide through nature itself. We can observe how the birds are busy picking around in the grass seeking insects, building their nest and providing for their offspring. For God, we are of much greater worth than the birds. If God provides for them isn't it then a sure thing that He will provide for your life?

Remember that you were created in His image, that you have value and that you were redeemed by the blood of His beloved Son. In this passage, Jesus emphasizes the need to fully trust in Him as provider.

If He takes care of something as fragile as a sparrow, how much more will He take care of you so that you lack nothing? If you believe this with all your heart it will be a tremendous help for weak faith. Don't allow economic needs to distract you from what God wants you to believe.

If He takes care of the birds, He will surely take care of you.

Jesus also teaches in this chapter that no one can add even one cubit to his height; this speaks of the vanity of human effort to sustain oneself (daily food and clothing) if God doesn't bless him. Jesus shows that true confidence is to seek first the Kingdom of God and His righteousness (and not seek the self righteousness which is in reality is a false righteousness from Mammon.)

To seek the Kingdom of God is the key to deport and defeat Mammon. When you make the will of God your main priority, you are the victor.

His teaching was that if He has taken care of something as fragile as the birds and has clothed the wild flowers with so much beauty and elegance with such great detail, how could He not consider mankind as more important for Himself?

The lesson is to understand that man should put as his priority the principles of the Kingdom of God.

There are laws in the Kingdom on how to obtain true riches. To seek His Kingdom and to put Him in first place above all else is sufficient to receive the fullness of all things, because if He takes care of the birds of the air, He will take care of me. The Kingdom of God is righteousness, peace and joy. To have Mammon as security ($) and money to attain these displaces God first place in the heart. *And thou shalt love the Lord thy God with all thy heart, and with all thy soul, and with all thy mind, and with all thy strength.* Without realizing it, Mammon can occupy the place that is intended to be only for God. To understand this more clearly we must understand the first and most important commandment which is to *love the Lord thy God with all thy heart, and with all thy soul, and with all thy mind, and with all thy strength.*

For that reason it is impossible to have Mammon in first place and then God. Jesus clearly said: *for either he will hate the one, and love the other.* Earlier in this same chapter Jesus spoke of walking totally in the light; this is to say that those who don't have Him in first place can walk partially in darkness. The in verse 21 He says: *For where your treasure is, there will your heart be also.*

God loves a cheerful giver; but there is a difference between giving out of the revelation of the need to give and to give to get in return. Christ wants us to give happily because of who He is, the God we can always trust. He sees the intentions of the heart with the greatest detail.

Jesus was addressing the important issue that man must analyze very carefully who really makes the decisions within him. The fact that we are already children of God and no longer slaves makes us prosperous and blessed. If we seek His Kingdom first, the blessings will follow us automatically. The important factor to consider is to change the order of our priorities. His righteousness, peace and joy must come first along with the principle of the Kingdom. Clothes, food and the necessary things of life come afterwards. God blesses through our work done correctly! He has promised to give us the intelligence to develop riches through the grace deposited within us. God has promised to bless the work of diligent hands.

The rich young man left sadly

The young man saith unto him, All these things have I kept from my youth up: what lack I yet? Jesus said unto him, If thou wilt be perfect, go and sell that thou hast, and give to the poor, and thou shalt have treasure in heaven: and come and follow me. But when the young man heard that saying, he went away sorrowful: for he had great possessions. Then said Jesus unto his disciples, Verily I say unto you, That a rich man shall hardly enter into the kingdom of heaven. Matthew 19:20-23

Jesus will not compromise His truth with Mammon. The rich young man loved his riches more than he loved the commandments and the will of God. He had knowledge of the commandments but in his heart they were in second place.

There is still one thing you must do was the answer Jesus gave him. One thing and he couldn't enter the Kingdom of God? Because of only one thing he couldn't deny himself? For this rich young man the issue was his possessions. Jesus was radical; the "mammon" of this man was his possessions, houses and lands. Jesus told him to sell all that he had in order to follow Him and to attain the promised blessings of the Kingdom of

God. Doesn't it seem that Jesus was being a little hard on him? Perhaps Jesus wasn't thinking about all the good personal qualities of this young man.

Jesus will allow you to go, falling in love with Mammon little by little. But you will lose Him in the process, just as the rich young man lost his opportunity to enter the Kingdom of God.

Today the image of this young man would be different. It would be something like this: a talented man with a good image, good position and apt for leadership. Who here is mistaken? Christ or our modern way of thinking? How many people are serving in churches today with the same mentality of the rich young ruler? But this doesn't guarantee that they will enter into the Kingdom of God.

The root of all evil is the love of money. God will not compete with Mammon, as he was defeated on the Cross of Calvary. He will however, allow you to choose.

What you love and have in first place in your heart will be manifested by your words and actions. A person might have riches, material riches, but that doesn't mean that that he has riches before God. (Luke 12:21)

REMEMBER, the world and money has a profound relation to the spiritual. If God the Creator is rich, won't His children be rich also? It is then to know the plans of God for your life. Once that you recognize the last Adam, (that destroyed the work of the first Adam on the Cross), your vision of work and finances will totally change. Adam was made a child of God with all the rights that are implied, do you consider yourself a child of God or not?

The prosperity of God is the perfect plan of the Creator for His children. We must go to the enemy's camp and take back what has stolen from us.

The revelation of the spirit of mammon

Tatiana Figueroa, one of the intercessors of the Jesus is Alive Today International Ministries and programming director of the television ministry of the JVH Network was praying at the altar of church during the time this book was being edited. While praying in the Spirit and seeking the Lord she suddenly had a revelation. This is how she shares it: *I sensed that the Lord was speaking to me. I had been praying for quite a while when I began to travail in the Spirit. I clearly began to understand the message that He wanted to give me: Money is spiritual, He said, because there is worship... The root of all evil is the love of money. Many are worshipping it as if it were a god and have built an altar for its worship, serving it as "lord."*

How is the god of this world served?

- Loving him
- Needing him
- Speaking of him
- Seeking him
- Thinking about him day and night
- Lusting after him
- Becoming sad when he is not there

Why is money spiritual? Because it is worshipped, venerated, coveted, taken care of, watched after and not shared. Money causes a breaking away from true worship and dependence on the Lord.

When does man worship money (perhaps without knowing it)? It is worshipped when Mammon takes control of the heart and becomes the lord of people's lives. It is then that man becomes its servant; when money becomes an idol and a god. He then determines when one can be happy and when not; he determines what is given, how much is given and when the time comes to shut off the flow. As he is a god (god of covetousness and temporal riches), he knows how to bring bondage, provoke dependence on him and cut off any way of escape. He delights seeing them before his throne as they tell him how much they need him and how happy they would be if he were in their lives. The Lord would say that there are those who yearn for times past when he was their god and not I.

There are many who are destroying their lives and marriages because he is ruling their lives deciding for them when and how they can live; they know that they can't stand life without him ($). God says that when they enthrone him in their hearts: "I am no longer there. When they worship him and seek him and no longer seek me, they are rejecting Me as the true source of their needs." Many rob the tithe and refuse to give offerings because they can't tolerate seeing their resources diminish. The characteristics of the worshipers of Mammon are these: self centered, controlling and manipulative, ambitious, covetous and lying.

I (Tatiana) saw him when I was at the altar; he was fat and black for the darkness in him. He had earrings in his ears and nose; he has a large belly.

The Lord told me: "This is the god that many serve today; because of him many been corrupted and have twisted My Word and have abandoned Me for a cheap doctrine."

I stood up and even though I began to pray, I started to write what I was hearing which is this:

Mammon determines what kind of life his followers have because he is a god and lord. He throws leftovers and crumbs to his followers as a cheap imitation of God's Word. He throws crumbs imitating Jesus, but the difference is that He, Jesus, crowns us with mercy and favor.

How can we dethrone him from our lives?

- **Tear him down:** When we tear him down we put on the power of the Name of the Lord Jesus; we put him under our feet and take authority over him by the Blood of Jesus. (Christ took authority over all principalities triumphing over them publicly on the Cross.)
- **Take him out** of the place that we ourselves put him in. If there was a generational family issue that put him on the throne he may move more freely

without us even realizing it, he then is more camouflaged and avoids detection because he is a familiar spirit. In Colombia (my country of origin) it is not uncommon to hear about pacts done with witchcraft for the family business that have prospered. But behind this there are curses of death, kidnappings, robbery and horribly frightening things that leave great pain and separation of loved ones.

Money is not an end but rather an instrument. It is a document created by man with the purpose of completing a financial transaction. Money should work for us, not us work for money. The power given to money must be taken away.

To those who are spiritual and as children of God we must be very careful not to venerate money or be carried away with the system of the world. We must replace that system with the real thing; God created gold and silver and as a result, we must trust in Him with all out heart. He is our supplier and helper. In this way, money will flow to us to cover our needs and make us abound for all good works.

How do we defeat the enemy and take away his power of control?

- By repentance
- By taking him captive
- By binding him
- By taking back what he stole from us
- By taking authority over him
- By bringing him into the light he no longer has power and control over our lives. He therefore must then release finances and resources so that they flow toward us; this is a spiritual issue.

God sees your heart and knows if it is genuine and transparent, if it is really detached from material possessions. He knows if the desire to have money is for good works and to extend His Kingdom. If things are aligned correctly He will honor you and He will allow you to have finances.

However, if we are still holding on to the god of this world, worshipping him and treating in a very special way because he is god. REMEMBER: if you pretend to do spiritual warfare without a pure heart, he will come against you and attack you from your blind side. Since he still has areas in you that are in darkness, this gives him access, control and power over you.

Please take this counsel with love:

- Become independent of him
- Conquer him and bind him with the authority of Christ binding him in the Name of Jesus. You warfare against him will be by giving more offerings and giving more to the Kingdom of God.
- Use money to extend the Kingdom of God on the earth. Money serves you; you do not serve money.

We must learn to be detached of the things on earth because when we release them form our heart there is a return with the blessing of God and superabundance from heaven. All this will flow more and more in you as it is spiritual. *The blessing of the Lord, it maketh rich, and he addeth no sorrow with it.* God bless you.

13
The Economics Of World Commerce

To understand what specifically moves behind the world economy we must first know about the development of commerce in general and its beginnings in world history. The Phoenicians were the first to do commerce by sea trade and were also the first to do business with the barter system. This was a simple method to exchange products to obtain new things that were no available in their countries.

Phoenicia was populated by 3,000 BC and located in the West coast of the Mediterranean Sea. Tyre, Sidon and Byblos were the three most important cities. Since its location was on the Mediterranean this gave rise to the building of popular ports.

Prosperous... Who, Me?

Of these Phoenician cities Tyre stood out as predominant for over 200 years. During the time of King Solomon, Hiram I became king of Tyre; these two enjoyed commercial interchange that included wood, land and cities.

For the king's ships went to Tarshish with the servants of Huram: every three years once came the ships of Tarshish bringing gold, and silver, ivory, and apes, and peacocks. And king Solomon passed all the kings of the earth in riches and wisdom. 2 Chronicles 9:21-22

Even though that Hiram I was an arrogant and opulent man, he knew how to lead his people to prosperity. He expanded commerce and the exchange of merchandise with other countries.

Even after Tyre was conquered the Phoenicians founded another city that according to the historians were able to oppose powerful invaders such as the Romans. The name of this city is Carthage, a name that means "New City." Its location was at the other extreme of the Mediterranean on the African coast.

Phoenician trade

The Phoenicians capitalized on their large forests

of cedar making it the basic element of the construction of their ships. They brought back precious cargo from Arabia that included essences, myrrh, gold and exotic precious stones, from Assyria they obtained porcelain and delicate pieces of finely worked ivory from China, fabrics, silk and cotton, from India they brought the highly sought after spices, fine wood and pearls. From the area of the Black Sea and what today is Spain they brought horses, from areas around the Aegean Sea they obtained marble that satisfied the fancies of kings and potentates of the entire known world who built their residences and palaces of this fine material. From Egypt came fine linen and great quantities of grains.

To be able to understand what was going on behind "commerce and trade" it is necessary to know what was going on behind their religious activities. They worshipped six regional gods that varied little from city to city. They erected great pantheons and their antagonistic gods were similar to those of the ancient religion of Babel, the city that was founded by Nimrod.

- They sacrificed humans to their god Moloch, preferably children.
- Before coming to an agreement in a business negotiation or embarking on a

voyage, the Phoenicians occasionally practiced hierogamy (which was temple prostitution with the purpose of practicing a religious fertility rite).
- They also dedicated diverse offerings to their gods imploring their help or looking to the stars or to the entrails of the sacrificed animals to ascertain the outcome of the business endeavor.
- It should not be surprising that the Phoenicians installed the shapes of horses in the bow of their ships as an amulet of protection; their ships also bore the insignia of a half moon which was the symbol of Ashtoreth. The logic was to surround themselves with divine protection before facing the dangerous seas.

The deities used behind trade

They adored heavenly bodies and especially the stars that guided their navigation by night. The Phoenician gods were connected with the power of the hostile gods that were originally from Babel and worshipped by certain ethnical Semites groups (these were related to the worship of heaven, earth and sea).

In first place were all those that had the attributes of the supreme god. These were linked to the astral king, that is, with the sun called "Baal." Baal was considered the guardian of trade and was seen as the symbol of sovereignty. His name is translated as "lord" or "master."

"Moloch" is next and was recognized as sovereign and king. Next was the revered lady of excellence whose generic name was Baalat and also know as Ashtoreth or Astarte, the moon goddess, fertility goddess, deity on the oceans, seas, rivers and springs. The Phoenicians erected altars in her honor and sculpted in the bows of their boats in the form of a bull or of a man with bull horns. In Carthage human sacrifices were offered to these, generally newborns that were burnt alive.

There were also the plant deities that died in winter and came back to life in spring, similar to the natural cycle. "Hathor" was assimilated from the Egyptians and was a feminine deity that represented the cosmos and linked to the veneration of the dead. She appeared as a woman with a cows head and elongated horns that held a solar disc. Today she is called the seafarers patron.

Today under other names these same deities continue to be worshipped in our modern society; those that venerate them have the hope of being protected, hidden and guarded. Others seek them for fame, riches or ostentatious properties.

- **Baal** is Satan himself that is worshipped by men by impersonating the Creator God. He is the supposed son of the Phoenician pantheon and is god of fame and riches.
- **Astarte** today is worshipped by the hired killers of Colombia; the drug dealers use her as the patron and protector of their business. In Mexico she is known as "the white girl" (La niña blanca), a virgin that is connected to death and protects the mercenaries; she is worshipped in jails for personal protection. She is also known as virgin mother of the universe, worshipped as panchamama, queen of the universe and of the harvests.
- **Moloch:** According to the Bible the people made human sacrifices of new born children to this deity. One of the largest mafia groups of the world exists by murder and the millions of dollars that are generated annually by abortion. This is sustained by organized crime that deals with millions of dollars.

- **Melqart** is the protector deity of commerce and of the city; he is called "the god of the city." The Greeks adopted this deity from the Phoenicians and gave him an identity with the name Hercules. (Today he is considered as the territorial strong man.) Also, he is known as one of the principal guardians of the mafia, trafficking of organs, children, prostitutes, weapons and drugs.
- **Dagon** in Phoenicia was a fertility god similar to Astarte that came from Babylon. Dagon was a sea god, half man (woman) and half fish. He had as his companion a goddess that today would be called a mermaid connected to enchantments, sex and lust.

There is still more and the list is innumerable, but, what do these deities worshipped by the fathers of ancient commerce have to do with modern commerce? These demonic principalities (deities) gave them greatness, protection and power, the very same thing that happens today.

The Book of Ezekiel speaks of the King of Tyre, a rich, opulent and majestic king. He is the typological representation of government power that is accompanied by worldly ostentations that are obtained by abundant riches and power. He also represents the prince of this world of those who follow his ways. God demands judgment on the city of Tyre for despising and mocking Jerusalem. (Ezekiel 26:2) The city of Tyre in the Bible represents economic and commercial power, fame, riches, luxury and splendor.

The prophet Isaiah also prophesied against this opulent city and the system of Tyre. (Isaiah 23:17-18) This judgment was to last 70 years but the curious thing here is that the prophecy also says Tyre will rise up again for international trade and fornication with the nations of the earth. This prophecy will once again be fulfilled at the beginning of the Tribulation. In Revelation the apostle John sees the world's economic systems crash at the fall of Babylon.

Therefore thus saith the Lord God; Behold, I will give the land of Egypt unto Nebuchadrezzar king of Babylon; and he shall take her multitude, and take her spoil, and take her prey; and it shall be the wages for his army. I have given him the land of Egypt for his labour wherewith he served against it, because they wrought for me, saith the Lord God. In that day will I cause the horn of the house of Israel to bud forth, and I will give thee the opening of the mouth in the midst of them; and they shall know that I am the Lord. Ezekiel 29:19-21

This will be the end of the world economic system and of those who placed their trust in temporal riches.

God gave no payment or plunder for fulfilling to Tyre for fulfilling the prophecy. God kept the riches for His own purposes. This means that there will be transference of wealth for the King and His Kingdom when He establishes His Glory in the earth; the nations will bring all their wealth to Jesus the Messiah; He will be honored and magnified as the only wise God and King of Kings forever.

Satan behind world wide extortion

In our time there are huge multimillion dollar movements that owe their power to demon worship, among these are:

- **The Mafia** This is a term that is used through the world to refer to a special class of organized crime that extended from its origin in Italy and is used for any group that has similar characteristics

independently of their origin or geographical operations.
- **Drug trafficking** This worldwide illegal industry deals with the cultivation, manufacture, distribution and sale of illegal drugs.
- **The black market or underground economy** This term is used to describe the clandestine sale of products, goods or services that violate price fixing or taxes imposed by the government. Countries that prohibit, restrict or allow the elevated pricing of tobacco or alcohol bring about the appearance of those who introduce these products illegally. This also includes the buying and selling of drugs and weapons.
- **Holy Death or The Little White Girl** Worship and prayer is offered to a skeletal figure which is part of a Mexican cult, this figure receives requests for luck, money and protection as well as evil intended petitions to harm others. For the most part, these followers are considered delinquents, drug traffickers and thieves.
- **Terrorism** is the activation or threat of power through the use of violence, assassinations, torture, kidnapping of civilians and the extortion of their

properties by individuals or organized groups not duly appointed by any government agency to coerce and thereby obtain political or religious – political ends.
- **Organized Crime** These are socially organized communities that develop criminal activities to earn money. These activities are usually the trafficking of drugs, weapons, replicas of paintings or of archaeological treasures. The majority of these communities have a hierarchical order and the common forms expressions are usually gangs or mafia.
- **The Triad Society** This is a generic term that used to designate certain Chinese criminal organizations that have their base in Hong Kong, Taiwan and continental China along with sectors of the Diaspora Han. These groups deal in the falsification of credit cards, clandestine shops, sale and distribution of all kinds of products, prostitution, illegal clinics and murder for hire. They sell heroine in the United States that comes form their fields in Thailand and Laos and launder the money in other countries.
- **The Pyramid Scheme** These are known as the circle of prosperity on the wheel of friendship, etc. This is criminal deception

and fraud that has many names and is extending through Latin America, United States, the Caribbean and Spain. The pyramid scheme is a model of business that is non-sustainable that involves earning money primarily on enrolling others in the scheme without receiving products or services. These schemes take advantage of naïve people and the confusion between the legal system and others systems that have the end of deceiving people.

- **Identity Theft** is the fastest growing crime in the world. Until recently when a thief stole a wallet or documents, these were his only objective. This is changing; now its much more important to have the number on the document, the credit card, debit card, checking account or any other document that contains personal information. During the course of a normal day, you give this information when you complete a transaction in person, by phone or online when you purchase a product or service. If this confidential information falls in the hands of a delinquent, he could use it steal your financial identity and perform many of your activities in your name.

These are other activities that have the same undertones and background:

- casinos and games of random luck
- lottery
- laundering money
- robbery
- fraud
- looting
- theft, swindling and extortion

14
Revealing the Hidden Government (NWO)

Understand clearly that everything that has happened and will happen has been outlined by God. God has allowed Satan to rule for a time so that everything that has been written in His Word through the prophets will be fulfilled. The new world order wants to establish itself all over the face of the earth. As part of the initial plan the idea is to put all people on the same level in the creation a new world order of economy, politics and religion.

We should understand that the term new world order first of all is not new and secondly will never be orderly.

Prosperous... Who, Me?

For thousands of years there have been very well elaborated projects by secret societies to subtly influence world events.

The expression **"New World Order"** has been used to refer to a new period in history where there is evidence of dramatic changes in political ideology and the balance of power. This phrase was used cautiously at the end of the Second World War when the plans were being described of the creation of the United Nations and the Bretton Woods Agreements, due to the negative association that resulted from the failure of the League of Nations.

The New World Order is a plan designed by Adam Weishsaupt, creator of the Illuminati which fits into the modern conspiracy theories. According to these conspiracy theories, the NWO is a plan whose purpose is to overthrow the governments and kingdoms of the world, to eradicate from the earth (if it were possible) every fundamentalist Christian, to eliminate all religions and beliefs to unify mankind un a "new order" of politics, religion and economics; this way all people would attain perfection.

One of the variants of the modern conspiracy theories is the process of "globalization" which began in the beginnings of the twentieth century over the whole planet. The commencement of the meetings of the G-7 and later of the G-8 and the present day G-20 is world globalization carried out in secret meetings. This group with its diverse members comes from politicians, bankers and royalty, the most influential people in the world who meet annually under high levels of secrecy.

The hidden world government

Its difficult to imagine that in a society like our of today that human beings could be subject to powerfully organized forces designed to run their lives, manipulate their desires and order their thoughts. An extensive world organization comprised of corporations and associations that are apparently altruistic, cultural and ecological watches over and controls the civic reactions of the inhabitants of planet earth.

There is an unseen government that runs the world above the individual national states. The great statesman, Benjamin Disraeli said: **"The world is governed by people very different than what commonly is believed by those that can't see farther than their own eyes."**

Lenin also affirmed this by saying: **"Behind the October revolution there are many figures much more influential than the thinkers and executors of Marxism."**

Sir Winston Churchill assured that **"he that does not see that in the earth a great undertaking is progressing, an important plan that doesn't allow the collaboration of faithful servants for its achievement must certainly be blind."**

A reporter for the Washington Post asked ex-President George Bush what would happen after the fall of the Soviet Union. He replied: **"What we say goes."**

Franklin D. Roosevelt declared: **"In politics nothing is casual. If something happens, be sure that it was planned that way."**

It is hard to imagine that the world of today was planned in the time of Christopher Columbus and that the French and Russian Revolution, Nazism and the Communist age are links in a chain of events brought about by men that think they have power over the cosmic laws of polarization.

In 1776 consumerism did not exist, the concept was not even known in a world where misery and poverty were the norm. However, in one of the proceedings of the occult society called "The League of Just Men" which was formed that same year we find this: **"the bitter struggle for the goods that money can buy generates a society without a heart."** We see that this has become a present day reality after more that 200 years, a plan with the purpose of subjugating man and all of humanity.

A capitalist conspiracy based on the dominance of money was founded over a century ago when Barron Rothschild, a renowned international banker that financed Napoleon, made this famous statement: **"give me the control of the money and it will no longer matter who rules or writes the laws."** Could it be that the International Monetary Fund (IMF) has taken these words seriously?

John Todd, who belongs to the Masonic "Council of 13", in the magazine "Progress for All" from January 1991, in an interview regarding the clarification of the Pyramid and the shining eye on the back of the US One Dollar Bill stated this: "The seal of the pyramid was created by the Rothschild family and brought to North America by Benjamin Franklin and Alexander Hamilton before 1776." The Rothschild family is the head of an organization which is at the head of all the Occult Brotherhoods. It is a Lucifer Organization to install his reign in the whole world. The eye on the pyramid is the eye of Lucifer.

Franklin and Hamilton are the founders of the United States which declared its independence in 1776 at about the same time that Adam Weishaupt founded the League of Just Men in Germany.

Is it a coincidence that of the 56 men that signed the Declaration of Independence that at least 50 were Masons and that the 55 members of Constitutional Convention were as well? These facts are evident in American history and anyone can research this.

The demonic association of the Illuminated Ones appears for the first time in a document signed by Albert Pike on June 4, 1889 and has a decree of instructions directed to the 23 Supreme Councils of the Illuminati: **"To you, Sovereign Instructors of Grade 33, we tell you: you have to repeat to the brothers of inferior grades that we worship only one God to whom we pray without superstition. It is we, Initiated in the Supreme Grade, that are to keep the real**

Masonic religion preserving pure the Lucifer doctrine."

A document that was published sometime between 1901 and 1906 called "The Protocols of the Wise Men of Zion" and was also know as the "Testament of Satan." The British Museum in London has a copy of the document. These are selected phrases from this Testament: **"Those that seduce the people with political and social ideas are subject to our yoke. Their unattainable utopias are undermining the prestige of national governments and the pillars of the present state of law."** **"When the people become disillusioned by their governments they will begin to cry out for a Unified Government that could bring peace and harmony; that will be the moment to enthrone our sovereign leader."**

The disenchantment of the citizens and the lack of credibility of the politicians that is seen today in any part of the world fit in perfectly with the plan that of those who at the beginning of the last century were seeking to implement this.

It seems that we have come to the time of the revelation of the world government leaders. What possibility was there that the League of Just Men could have seen what would happen a century later? This is very simple, they didn't just see it, they planned it with concrete objectives. Read the following:

"After discrediting the monarchies we will elect presidents among those that can be submissive servants. Those elected must have some dark aspect in their past so it can be easy to threaten them with being exposed by us. At the same time they will be bound to the power of their acquired position and enjoy the honors and privileges of being president; they will be anxious to cooperate as to not lose what they have attained." We shouldn't have to think too much to realize that this is true.

The one world government

In general we think that the concept of a one world government is new and that in the Maastricht Treaty this idea was incorporated into the European project. However, the idea is not new in Europe, this is a project that goes back to the League of Just Men and has been advancing under the power of international money.

Several years ago J. Warburg, a banker associated with the Rothschild and the Rockefellers announced before the American Senate: **"Like it or not, we will have a one world government. The question is only if it will come by consent or by force."**

What kind of government is being planned?

Zbigniew Brzezinski, the ex president of the Trilateral Commission declared the following: "It will be a technocratic era in which the prevailing ideal will be a reasonable humanitarianism on a world scope."

The word humanitarianism has a more complicated meaning that appears as the concept is defined as "a principle that denies the divine characteristics of Christ." This is a doctrine that determines human moral and ethical obligations are limited to the individual and individual relationships with no dependence on any other thing except for the satisfaction of desires and passions. (As the religion of the new millennium, the New Age preaches these philosophies.)

With this doctrine that morality doesn't exist, that God has died and that "religion is the opium of the people" we can sum up what has been preached by politicians and philosophers for the last one hundred and fifty years.

Z. Brzezinski declared in the magazine Encounter the following: "The technocratic age is slowly designing a society ever more controlled and that will be controlled by an elite group of people with traditional values that will not hesitate to obtain their objectives through purging techniques by which they will influence the behavior of the people; they will control and supervise every detail of society." And then he says: **"it will be possible to exercise an almost permanent surveillance over every citizen of the world."**

Money and Power

To move the immense machinery that is needed to control all of humanity requires billions of dollars and an extensive human and social infrastructure as well as an organization that controls the communication and the flow of information.

What is this infrastructure like and where does the money come from?

The network of conspirators that pulls the invisible strings throughout the entire world is comprised of bankers and international capitalists; they come from the mountaintops of international finance. They gather around themselves an army of scientists, technocrats, politicians and puppet agents that do their bidding from the shadows of obscurity.

Gary Allen also gives us ample information and shows that: "the international economic empires are interested in promoting the indebtedness of the governments." Continuing he shares: The higher the debt, the higher the interest. But also the presidents can be required to turn over fiscal privileges, force the monopoly of services and channel huge contracts at will. If these terms are not accepted, they will provoke their fall, promote disturbances and labor strikes that impoverish the nation and obliges them to bow to whatever they require."

In the United States the CFR is known as the Ministry of Rockefeller Affairs and as The Invisible Government of the World. It is the agency that tells the governments of the world what they must do. To think that the electors actually elect a government is totally illusory. A delegate of the CFR said: "It doesn't matter who the people votes for because they always vote for us." (Is it because of this that the winner of an election is known even before the votes are counted?)

In politics, as Roosevelt said, "nothing is by accident." It is evident in light of the "Testament of Satan" that what is happening now has been planned two hundred years ago. Today the Club of Rome, the CFR, the Trilateral Commission, the International Monetary Fund (IMF) and the Maastricht Treaty all follow the same objectives.

The evil is found in the fact that money has been converted into the unattackable protagonist of politics and societies to actively maintain their power over any other ethical or moral principle of the people. It is also found in the fact that the governments are burdened with the conflict of social welfare and helping the poor and the unavoidable collection of taxes.

The wrong is also found in the need to satisfy the polarization of social demands and claims, the governments that get into debt paying ever increasing interest to the Invisible Government of the Illuminated Ones. It is not hard to see behind the benevolent appearance of the system a diabolical plan is hidden that intends to take the power form the governments and put into the hands of the financiers.

Those supposedly illuminated in this text assure us that: "we have been elected by God Himself to rule the world. Even though some heroic spirit arises to stop us, he will not be able to face trained warriors such as us; he will have arrived too late." Supposing that this peril does come to pass, the illuminated ones are achieving one of their principal objectives and that of a society without a heart. In exchange for material things, we disdain the spiritual values of our society for modern "golden calves."

A plan is being elaborated that will be brought to fruition. What began as a project today is being transformed into an obvious reality. We can give a broad overview of the plan using the following categories with their respective lists.

Economic factors:

- the generalization of strikes
- the financial crisis of 1929
- the struggle of the classes
- the creation of the new economic science
- the arrogance of trusts and monopolies
- land speculation
- the arms race

- the progressive growth of state bureaucracy
- the progressive decline in the value of national currencies
- gold as the standard
- the appearance of a one world currency
- the progressive taxing of inheritances
- the current financial crisis
- the progressive disappearance of paper money and checks taking its place are credit cards and smart cards

Social factors:

- the rise of alcoholism and tobacco
- drugs
- youth delinquency
- the immense rise of power of the media
- the dismantling of morality
- the manipulation of public opinion
- the progressive disappearance of the family unit
- state control of education
- press associations and the qualifications of the informants
- the legalization of the professional secrecy for reporters
- the rise of gambling

- the explosion of professional sports
- the increase of prostitution legal o not
- the legalization of abortion

Religious factors

- the attack against Christianity and the attempt to erase the concept of God from the mind
- the vigorous opposition of professions of faith the produce atheists
- the promotion of religious dissidence
- the development of free thought, skepticism, religious debates, slighting religious hierarchies, ridiculing the personal habits of the faithful and more
- discrediting ministers before their faithful followers to diminish their influence and prestige
- opposition in Christian countries
- criticizing the Church without a direct attack

Moral factors

- The end justifies the means.

- We have to do what must be done for our advantage even if that means corruption, deceit and treason for the triumph of our cause.
- Against an enemy it is not immoral to use any means to defeat him.
- The number of victims that fall along the way doesn't matter as long as we have attained our goal.
- We have an ambition without limit, a devouring greed, a desire for vengeance without mercy and accumulated hate.

The pinnacle of this plan is to bring all people and nations under a one world government which includes a world economic system. Today there are five powerful and very dangerous forces that will hit the world economy with the impact of a train that is out of control.

1. The bank crisis
2. Deficit
3. Commercial and personal debt
4. Recession and depression
5. Renewed massive inflation.

All this will without a doubt give place to the establishment of a one world bank that is

orchestrated and organized by the global economic system.

Today people are running around all over the place for fear of what Jesus declared in Luke 21:26: *Men's hearts failing them for fear, and for looking after those things which are coming on the earth: for the powers of heaven shall be shaken.*

What the Bible says:

The Bible is considered the Word of God and inspired by the Spirit of God who moved upon the prophets as they wrote. In the Word we find the events that happened through the ages with precise accuracy and those that are still to come.

The organizers of this plan pretend to bring an earthly paradise to mankind but the Bible tells us that it will not occur. In the book written by the prophet Daniel and in Revelation written by John the apostle, we find the story of several world events, some of which happened in the past and others are yet to come. If what has been read up to now seems to be just a coincidence, those behind the plan are actively hoping for just the opposite.

They consider Lucifer as their god rejecting Jesus as the true Son of the living God. This goes back to the Cross of Calvary where the Messiah was not considered by the Jews as the savior of souls as they were expecting a social and economic liberator from the oppression of Rome. Well, the pseudo messiah will soon come by the hand of these worshippers of evil and the man of sin as the Bible calls him is about to show himself at any moment. A process of peace is desperately needed and apparently there is not even one world leader that can bring the peace that so many are dreaming of.

Please pay close attention as I will share with you who this person truly is according to the Scriptures. He is called the Antichrist, together with the Beast and the False Prophet they are the diabolical trinity whose number is 666. The future World Leader will definitely be possessed by Satan. If you do not believe this remember that Hitler who with sadism, perverse and diabolical subtlety declared himself to be involved in a satanic association that developed its strategy by consulting with demons. His great hatred led him to try to destroy the Jewish race, God's chosen people.

God will allow the Antichrist to exercise his authority for seven years. During the first three and one half years he will woo the masses making them think that they will live in a world of peace and tranquility. But in the last three and one half years he will come against those who brought him into power and make himself pass as god, seating himself in the place reserved only for the true God. He will also impose order in that those who do not take a mark on their hand or forehead will not be able to buy or sell. He that does not worship him as god will be unmercifully killed; doing what he commands will be in effect will be surrendering the soul to Satan.

Money will no longer exist; this system can be implemented today with all the technological advances. There are also unstoppable advances of science that will force the use of a microchip placed under the skin on the hand or the forehead. This chip can contain millions of bits of personal information such as bank accounts and wages deposited, etc. With the pass of the hand or forehead with a scanner a caramel or a car can be purchased.

There are so many important things, God tells us that the Antichrist will be wounded in the head and for three days will be dead. He will rise for the dead to the amazement of the people and will be considered as the true god. This satanic act is to imitate Jesus in His death and resurrection. As we can see, the future of the world is not pleasant. But there is hope which is in Christ. If we have the faith that He died and rose from the dead so that we can be saved, He can be our personal **Savior**.

Remember that while we are seeing the fulfillment of all these things the steps of the Lord are being heard in the hallway of eternity. We are living in the end times.

Part 5

True Riches

15
Temporal and Eternal Riches

Temporal riches

The world has fallen uncontrollably under the seduction of false security and economic instability. Before our eyes the throne of riches is falling apart while at the same time millions have been seized by the power of Mammon becoming increasingly dependent upon him, greedy and falling into the bottomless pit of ambition. (The more one has the more one wants.)

Wilt thou set thine eyes upon that which is not? For riches certainly make themselves wings; they fly away as an eagle toward heaven. Eat thou not the bread of him that hath an evil eye, neither desire thou his dainty meats: Proverbs 23:5-6.

This text mentions the greedy miser. This is he who is bound by a spirit of avarice; this is the extremely greedy person that hoards possessions as to become rich and won't release money as to meet a need.

Instead of becoming exhausted in the pursuit of riches, the Scriptures exhort us to seek after the Wisdom of God and what glorifies Him.

There is a sore evil which I have seen under the sun, namely, riches kept for the owners thereof to their hurt. Ecclesiastes 5:13

The treasures of this earth are temporary, bring certain disadvantages, produce anxiety and pain and can disappear because of poor administration. These people are those who have a superficial commitment without a true repentance as they cannot break with the love of money and of the world from which they came.

There are those who consider God as the only source of their riches; they understand that they may fully enjoy riches under the blessing of His presence.

The Word of God says: *He also that received seed among the thorns is he that heareth the word; and the care of this world, and the deceitfulness of riches, choke the word, and he becometh unfruitful. Matthew 13:22*

Charge them that are rich in this world, that they be not highminded, nor trust in uncertain riches, but in the living God, who giveth us richly all things to enjoy; That they do good, that they be rich in good works, ready to distribute, willing to communicate; Laying up in store for themselves a good foundation against the time to come, that they may lay hold on eternal life. 1 Timothy 6:17-19

REMEMBER: the word "highminded" means to have an exaggerated opinion or exceptionally high self esteem. Those that have great abundance tend to have contempt for others and that they are superior to them. They forget about the source of their possessions and that they are merely stewards of what God has given them to administrate.

It is important to understand that God is able to provide or furnish riches much greater than what can come from any earthly investment.

Riches and pride almost always walk hand in hand; the greater the empowerment greater is the temptation is to fall into pride. The cause is that they tend to trust their riches and the power of their abilities.

The apostle Paul recommends to Timothy what should be taught saying that those who are rich in material things, those who have more than the essential should be good stewards of the riches that God has given them. That means they should be generous, giving and investing so that the Word of God is taken and millions have the opportunity to know Jesus.

Judas Iscariot and riches

While I was with them in the world, I kept them in thy name: those that thou gavest me I have kept and none of them is lost, but the son of perdition; that the scripture might be fulfilled. John 17:12

Judas Iscariot after having been in the presence of His creator was lost, and for only thirty pieces of silver. Judas was one of the twelve disciples. There was nothing strange in Judas except for the love of money. He was the treasurer of the group of disciples that was with Jesus and had as his responsibility the bag of money which belonged to all of the disciples. Why did Jesus give Judas the position of treasurer knowing that his weakness was money?

Sometimes God will allow you to be in key positions to test your heart. Either you get rid of excess baggage or the darkness will catch up with you and take you completely.

Judas was not interested in the poor but the money bag really caught his attention. Many times he appeared to be religious but he couldn't hide his critical and derogatory attitude especially next to the righteous acts of Jesus.

When a person is a perfectionist that always exposes the defects of others, insecurity hides in the bottom of his heart.

This he said (Judas), not that he cared for the poor; but because he was a thief, and had the bag, and bare what was put therein. John 12:6 Judas loved money and this opened a door through which Satan entered into him. Judas caused this sin to be the root of all evil.

1 Timothy 6:9-12 says: *But they that will be rich fall into temptation and a snare, and into many*

foolish and hurtful lusts, which drown men in destruction and perdition. For the love of money is the root of all evil: which while some coveted after, they have erred from the faith, and pierced themselves through with many sorrows. But thou, O man of God, flee these things; and follow after righteousness, godliness, faith, love, patience, meekness. Fight the good fight of faith, lay hold on eternal life, whereunto thou art also called.

Those who are determined to choose the riches of this world trusting only in money have lost their sense of priorities. They follow after those who did likewise: Balaam, Gehazi, Judas, Ananias and Sapphira along with millions more that add themselves to the list through out time.

Certainly the love of money is the root of all evil. How lamentable it is to realize that upon entering into the Kingdom of God many have come face to face with this sin and prefer to disobey the Lord for the love of money! Those who choose the way of the riches of this world trusting that their money will provide an escape from the tribulations of life are terribly mistaken. In the end, we will all be confronted in one way or another and great riches will not be the escape route.

Temporal riches are not everything in this life. There is powerful deception in the love of money; it is most certainly the root of all evil to loose touch with what are true riches while rushing blindly into the future with a high grade of uncertainty and insecurity.

One of the evidences of the rule of the Antichrist is the unrestrained love of money along with unbridled egoism and ambition for the material and passing things of life.

The world government and the massive conspiracy of the end times will be controlled by the rampant and absolute abandon to the love of money, the strength of the power behind the idolatry. Today a larger part of humanity, including a large part of the people that acknowledge the Lord, live their lives deceived and trapped by the destructive tentacles of the temporal riches of life.

It concerns the wise to correctly understand what true riches are and what priorities are those that God has clearly marked in His Word saying:

But seek ye first the kingdom of God, and his righteousness; and all these things shall be added unto you. Matthew 6:33 Jesus established that through seeking salvation the complete provision of God was to be enjoyed.

Remember: God always wants to prosper you according to His infinite resources which are more than can be imagined, not according to a certain measure based on your personal economy.

But my God shall supply all your need according to his riches in glory by Christ Jesus. Philippians 4:19 One of the perspectives about personal possessions is that they be used to honor God. This is attained by trusting in Him, generously giving first and the best to Him and by expressing gratitude for what He has given. The result of this faithfulness to honor Him with possessions will bring prosperity and satisfaction.

Permanent riches

I would like to share with the readers the Word that God gave me when I was studying about Mammon. (Pastor Lidia Zapico, November 2008)

Praying and studying about the spoils and plunder of war and how to get them, I asked the Lord: "After each battle is won, what part of the plunder will be mine?" He responded to my spirit, "Who won the battle?" I answered Him: "Evidently you did Lord, not me, of course." He said: "Therefore the plunder is mine; but out of this plunder I have taken gifts that have been distributed to men." "What then is my gift" I replied. "Wisdom, I will make you wise. Perhaps you prefer treasure that can be lost? Or do you prefer vain illusions? My treasures are more than this, more than precious stones. What I have I give you, my grace, favor and power. Behold, what the natural man does not consider valuable is what I consider as priceless and has eternal consequences. The riches of my grace are more than sufficient for the one who has achieved wisdom. In maturity wisdom is found, that which the foolish have despised. My riches, glory and honor come together with wisdom and maturity similar to the life of Solomon. He asked me for wisdom and riches were also part of his answer."

"Mammon does not lend or give anything with no strings attached. The souls that honor him are bound to him, their payment is deception, blind eyes and a distorted concept of eternity; what's worse is they forfeit their eternal life. They can only see the natural, their senses don't allow for real personal and spiritual development. Their wisdom is limited, carnal and earthly. Therefore they cannot see the hidden true riches. **There are temporal riches and there are permanent riches.** There is a difference between the two and to take away all confusion out of the mind my children must dig deeper into the Word. This will bring wisdom."

"I have left impressions in your spirit so you can learn to discover the hidden treasures, the knowledge of God that is concealed. My wisdom is a fountain without end or limits. Today everything that can be shaken will be shaken so that what is immovable remains because it was created to endure."

"For you, what are the precious pearls without price? For the wise one the riches of His grace are superior. But for each one that lives the normal life, everything is vanity. The only thing that will remain is the soul that has accumulated riches in heaven. Amen."

From a natural perspective the majority of people define riches as the abundance of possessions that have been accumulated. However, the Word of God teaches about the enduring riches that are different than most may think.

Temporal and Eternal Riches

Riches and honour are with me; yea, durable riches and righteousness. Proverbs 8:18

The enduring riches are those that He gives and are spiritual; they enrich the soul. These are the riches that allow us to be rich in God. It is true that spiritual riches are no recognized for their true worth but only by those that have not grown to use their senses based on the knowledge of the Word of God.

Let's look at the variety of great spiritual riches that are mentioned on the Word of God:

- The riches of His grace. (Ephesians 1:7-2:7, Ephesians 3:8, 16)
- The riches of His glory. (Ephesians 1:18, Philippians 4:19)
- The riches of generosity. (2 Corinthians 8:2)
- The riches of understanding. (Colossians 2:2)
- The riches of Christ in you. (Colossians 1:27)
- The riches of the reproach of Christ. (Hebrews 11:26)
- The riches of the glory of his inheritance in the saints. (Ephesians 1:18)

- The riches of full knowledge. (Colossians 2:2)

The riches of His grace

In whom we have redemption through his blood, the forgiveness of sins, according to the riches of his grace. Ephesians 1:7

In Christ we have the riches of true freedom. Through the favor obtained in Christ, the price was paid for the release and freedom of the captives. The sacrifice of Christ on the Cross of Calvary paid the price for their freedom; these are the redemptive riches of His grace. His redemption brought unlimited grace for the forgiveness of sins; there is nothing that can equal the value of the Blood of Jesus.

The riches of the glory in Christ

The eyes of your understanding being enlightened; that ye may know what is the hope of his calling, and what the riches of the glory of his inheritance in the saints. Ephesians 1:18

A mind that has knowledge and spiritual revelation can understand and appreciate the true hope and inheritance that we have in Christ. How important it is to the true riches of the glory that is to come!

The riches of full knowledge

That their hearts might be comforted, being knit together in love, and unto all riches of the full assurance of understanding, to the acknowledgement of the mystery of God, and of the Father, and of Christ; In whom are hid all the treasures of wisdom and knowledge. Colossians 2:2-3

It is clear that understanding, revelation and knowledge are extremely valuable gifts that not all people have the privilege to posses. The prophet Daniel had ten times the understanding of the scientists and fortune-tellers of his time in Babylon. God is the God of knowledge and fore knowledge which is knowing before it happens. In Him is all intelligence and wisdom, the treasures of the riches of full understanding.

The apostle Paul considered as rubbish all intellectual knowledge to be able to attain the wisdom that comes from above.

Paul declared that he had received this knowledge from the Spirit of God. He said that all the riches of truth that are necessary for salvation consists in the fact that He chose us for sanctification and to be glorified together with Him. Those that remain in sin and immaturity cannot perceive these riches. In 1 Corinthians 2:14-16 he says: *But the natural man receiveth not the things of the Spirit of God: for they are foolishness unto him: neither can he know them, because they are spiritually discerned. But he that is spiritual judgeth all things... But we have the mind of Christ.*

There are riches in the sufferings of Christ

Moses left Egypt the first fleeing to save his life as he feared the anger of Pharaoh. But the second time he left, he turned his back on Egypt and all it represented. *Esteeming the reproach of Christ greater riches than the treasures in Egypt: for he had respect unto the recompence of the reward. Hebrews 11:26* This time he didn't flee in fear but rather it was like God was so real that He was visible to his eyes, that He was actually watching him. This is a fundamental aspect of his loyalty to God, the true riches of what he had found in God. The strong faith of Moses did not allow him to doubt and he chose the reproach of suffering with his people instead of the temporal pleasure of what Egypt had to offer: entertainment, luxury of life in the palace, the charm and glitter of life in the big city. His faith allowed him to set his eyes on the reward. He left the temporal riches to receive the riches of God's glory.

The understanding of the love of God that is poured out in the heart of every mature Christian is what brings us into true spiritual treasures. These treasures open the heart to the deep wisdom and knowledge that spring up continually in the life of those who are in Christ.

Charge them that are rich in this world, that they be not highminded, nor trust in uncertain riches, but in the living God, who giveth us richly all things to enjoy; That they do good, that they be rich in good works, ready to distribute, willing to communicate. Laying up in store for themselves a good foundation against the time to come, that they may lay hold on eternal life. 1 Timothy 6:17-19

Riches are a responsibility. These texts clears up much regarding the poor understanding that exists about the acquisition and possession of material wealth. Paul tells us that we should not trust in what is uncertain. This refers to the insecurity that comes from trusting in temporal riches.

In this text the word "trust" comes from the Greek word *elpizo* which means simply hope or trust; to have a hope or trust in something. We should not put or trust in riches or hope that they bring us freedom or security.

Why does the apostle tell us that? It is because riches are transitory. Values in this world change and temporal riches represent a passing value. What is valuable today may not be valuable tomorrow. It would be wise then t deposit our hope and trust only in God and believe that He can provide for us.

Even more, we should never allow the possession of riches to make us believe that we are better than others or that we have the right to be irresponsible or negligent. It is a responsibility, a great responsibility to be the owner of great riches. We should always remember that he who has been given much, much will be required.

Paul encourages Timothy to tell those that are rich to **not be arrogant and place their hope in riches**. Only **the living God** can provide for our needs. Those who have riches are commanded to recognize the true source of their fortune and to be generous. Material blessings are to enjoy and use to advance the Kingdom, not just for personal pleasure.

The phrase "Laying up in store for themselves" could be translated as accumulating, a similar phrase is found in the challenge Jesus makes to lay up treasures in heaven. (Matthew 6:19-21) The believer's daily obedience to God builds a good foundation for what is to come. The scriptures teach that the works of the believer will be evaluated by what Christ produced in their lives.

Bibliography

The Arco Iris Study Bible. Reina-Valera Version, 1960 revision. Latin American Bible Society in Nashville. ISBN: 1-55819-555-6

Biblia Plenitud. Reina Valera Version, 1960. Editorial Caribe, Miami, Florida. ISBN: 089922279X

Vine's Complete Expository Dictionary of Old and New Testament Words. Editorial Caribe / Thomas Nelson, Inc. Nashville, TN. ISBN: 0-89922-495-4, 1999.

The Thompson Chain Reference Bible. Reina Valera Version 1960. Copyright 1987 The B.B. Kirkbride Bible Company, Inc. and Editorial Vida, Miami, FL ISBN: 0829714448 (From the original The Thompson Chain Reference Bible copyright ©1983

The MacArthur Study Bible © 1997 Word Publishing, Thomas Nelson, Inc. Nashville, TN

Strong's Exhaustive Concordance of the Bible. James Strong, LL.D., S.T.D. Editorial Caribe. ISBN: 0-89922-382-6

Wilkipedia The Free Encyclopedia 2009. Wilkipedia Foundation. August 10, 2004 http://wikipedia.org